Workbook for
Tonal Harmony

Workbook for

Tonal Harmony

with an Introduction to Twentieth-Century Music

Sixth Edition

Stefan Kostka
The University of Texas at Austin

Dorothy Payne
The University of South Carolina

McGraw-Hill
Higher Education

Boston Burr Ridge, IL Dubuque, IA New York San Francisco St. Louis
Bangkok Bogotá Caracas Kuala Lumpur Lisbon London Madrid Mexico City
Milan Montreal New Delhi Santiago Seoul Singapore Sydney Taipei Toronto

Mc Graw Hill **McGraw-Hill**
Higher Education

Workbook for Tonal Harmony

with an Introduction to Twentieth Century-Music

This book is printed on acid-free paper.

5 6 7 8 9 0 WDQ/WDQ 0

Cover: © James Jackson/Stockbyte

ISBN 978-0–07–332715–0
MHID 0–07–332715–8

http://www.mhhe.com

Contents

This icon denotes a listening example.

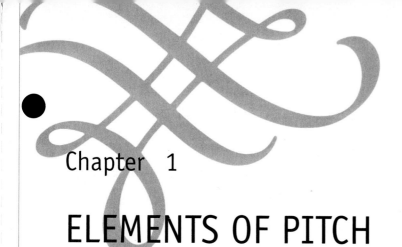

Chapter 1

ELEMENTS OF PITCH

EXERCISE 1–1

A. Name the pitches in the blanks provided, using the correct octave register designations.

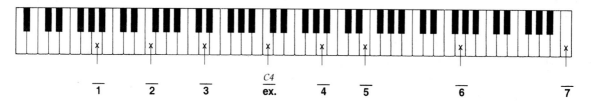

B. Notate the indicated pitches on the staff in the correct octave.

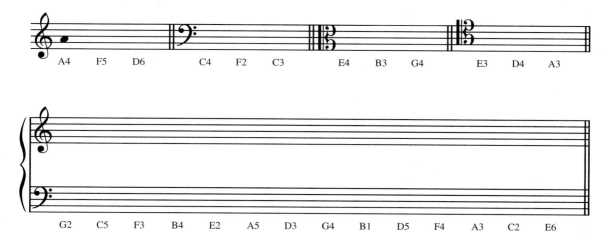

EXERCISE 1-2

A. Notate the specified scales using accidentals, not key signatures. Show the placement of whole and half steps, as in the example.

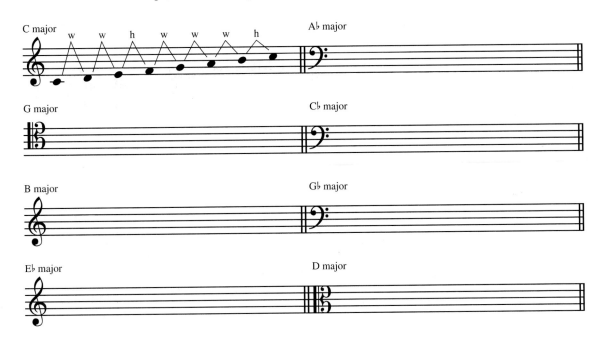

B. Identify these major key signatures.

_C_ major	_____ major	_____ major	_____ major	_____ major	_____ major	_____ major	_____ major
ex.	**1**	**2**	**3**	**4**	**5**	**6**	**7**

C. Notate the specified key signatures.

Ab major   E major   F major   C major

Gb major   G major   Eb major   C# major

). Fill in the blanks.

	Key signature	Name of key		Key signature	Name of key
1.	_____	D♭ major	**8.**	seven flats	_____ major
2.		G major	**9.**	_____	F major
3.	five sharps	_____ major	**10.**	_____	E major
4.	_____	E♭ major	**11.**	two sharps	_____ major
5.	two flats	_____ major	**12.**	three flats	_____ major
6.	three sharps	_____ major	**13.**	_____	G♭ major
7.	_____	C♯ major	**14.**	six sharps	_____ major

ll in the blanks, using the example as a model.

Major Key	Key Signature	Scale Degree	Is This Note
C	0♯/0♭	$\hat{5}$	G
E		$\hat{3}$	
_____	2♯	_____	C♯
_____	_____	$\hat{4}$	E♭
G♭	_____	_____	E♭
_____	3♯	$\hat{2}$	_____
_____	6♯	_____	C♯

ony

EXERCISE 1–3

A. Notate the specified scales using accidentals, not key signatures. The melodic minor
    should be written both ascending and descending.

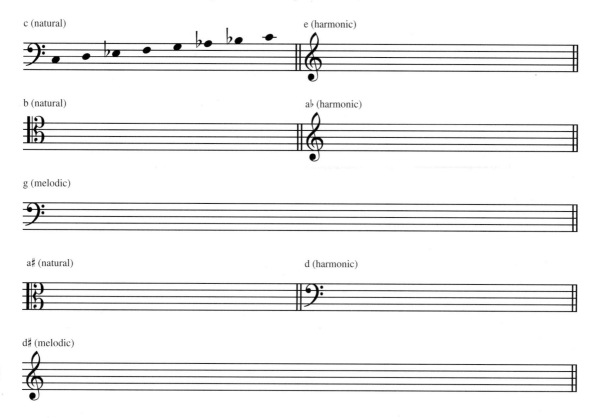

B. Identify the type of each scale as major, natural minor, harmonic minor, or melodic
    minor. Any melodic minor scales will be shown in the ascending version only.

C. Identify these minor key signatures.

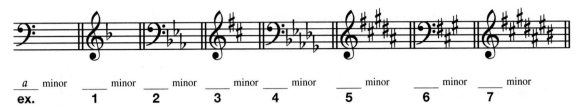

_a_ minor   ____ minor   ____ minor   ____ minor   ____ minor   ____ minor   ____ minor   ____ minor
ex.   **1**   **2**   **3**   **4**   **5**   **6**   **7**

D. Notate the specified minor key signatures.

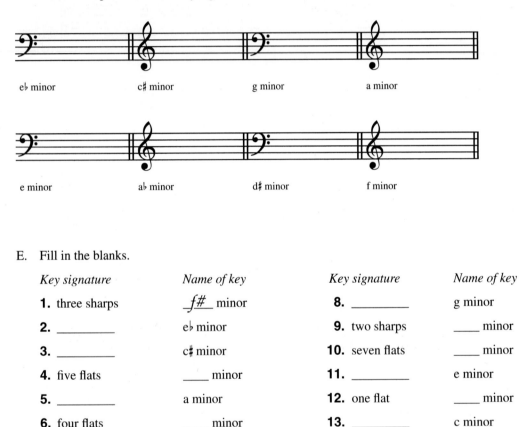

e♭ minor   c♯ minor   g minor   a minor

e minor   a♭ minor   d♯ minor   f minor

E. Fill in the blanks.

Key signature	*Name of key*	*Key signature*	*Name of key*
1. three sharps	_f♯_ minor	**8.** _____	g minor
2. _____	e♭ minor	**9.** two sharps	____ minor
3. _____	c♯ minor	**10.** seven flats	____ minor
4. five flats	____ minor	**11.** _____	e minor
5. _____	a minor	**12.** one flat	____ minor
6. four flats	____ minor	**13.** _____	c minor
7. seven sharps	____ minor	**14.** _____	g♯ minor

EXERCISE 1–4

A. Provide the numerical names of the intervals by using the numbers 1 through 8.

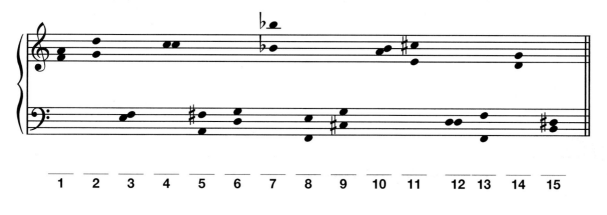

1 2 3 4 5 6 7 8 9 10 11 12 13 14 15

EXERCISE 1–5

A. All the following intervals are 4ths, 5ths, unisons, or octaves. Put a "P" in the space provided *only* if the interval is a perfect interval.

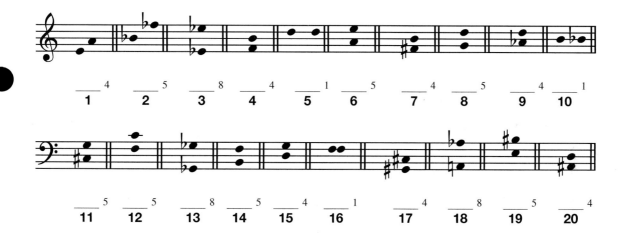

___4   ___5   ___8   ___4   ___1   ___5   ___4   ___5   ___4   ___1
  1   2   3   4   5   6   7   8   9   10

___5   ___5   ___8   ___5   ___4   ___1   ___4   ___8   ___5   ___4
 11   12   13   14   15   16   17   18   19   20

B. All the following intervals are 2nds, 3rds, 6ths, or 7ths. Put an "M" or an "m" in each space, as appropriate.

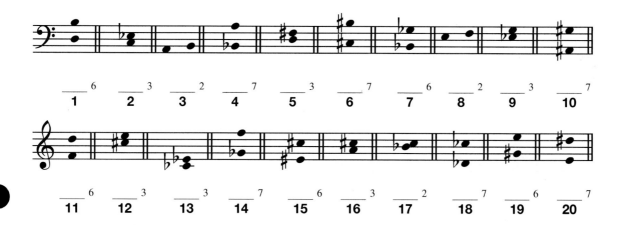

___6   ___3   ___2   ___7   ___3   ___7   ___6   ___2   ___3   ___7
  1   2   3   4   5   6   7   8   9   10

___6   ___3   ___3   ___7   ___6   ___3   ___2   ___7   ___6   ___7
 11   12   13   14   15   16   17   18   19   20

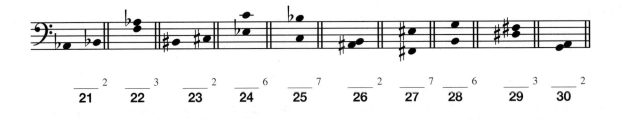

C. Notate the specified intervals above the given notes.

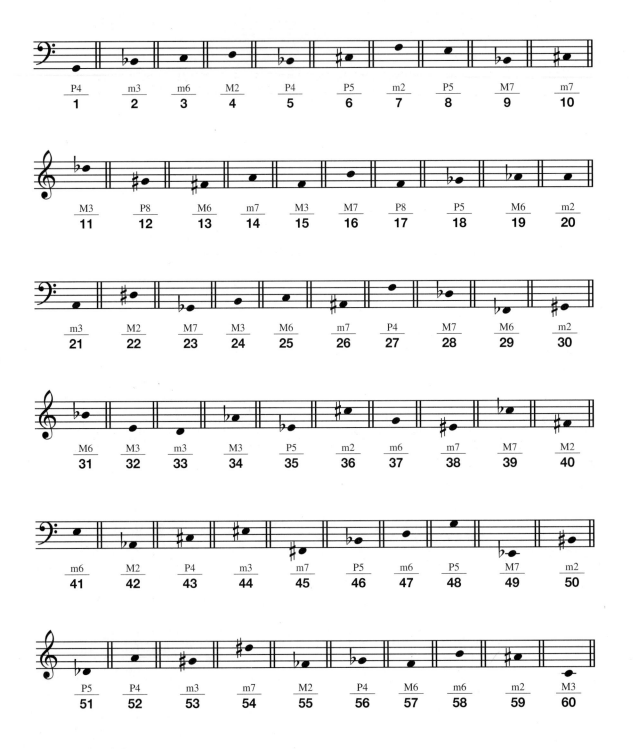

EXERCISE 1–6

A. Most of the intervals that follow are either augmented or diminished. Name each interval.

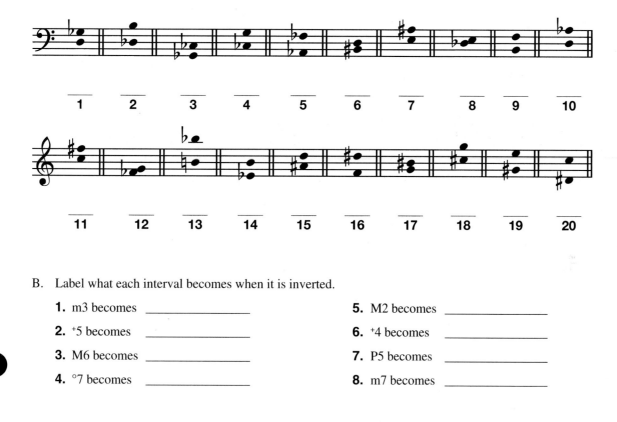

1	2	3	4	5	6	7	8	9	10

11	12	13	14	15	16	17	18	19	20

B. Label what each interval becomes when it is inverted.

1. m3 becomes _____
2. ⁺5 becomes _____
3. M6 becomes _____
4. °7 becomes _____

5. M2 becomes _____
6. ⁺4 becomes _____
7. P5 becomes _____
8. m7 becomes _____

C. Notate the specified interval *below* the given note. (You might find it helpful to invert the interval first in some cases.)

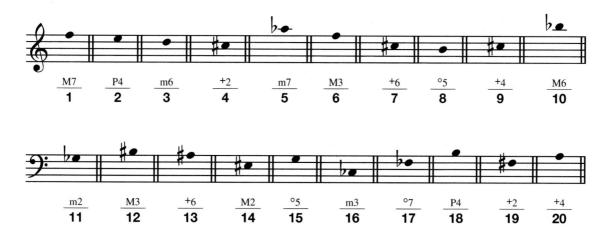

M7	P4	m6	+2	m7	M3	+6	°5	+4	M6
1	2	3	4	5	6	7	8	9	10

m2	M3	+6	M2	°5	m3	°7	P4	+2	+4
11	12	13	14	15	16	17	18	19	20

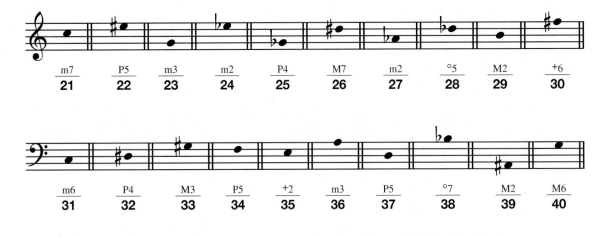

m7	P5	m3	m2	P4	M7	m2	°5	M2	+6
21	**22**	**23**	**24**	**25**	**26**	**27**	**28**	**29**	**30**

m6	P4	M3	P5	+2	m3	P5	°7	M2	M6
31	**32**	**33**	**34**	**35**	**36**	**37**	**38**	**39**	**40**

D. Label each interval in this melody (from Wagner's *Götterdämmerung*).

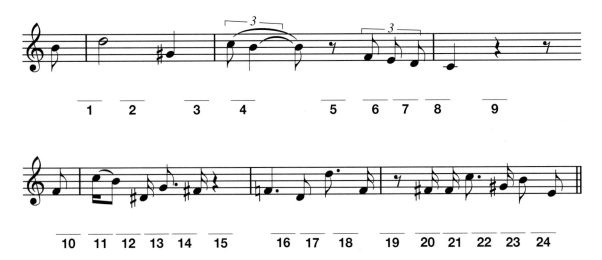

1	2	3	4	5	6	7	8	9

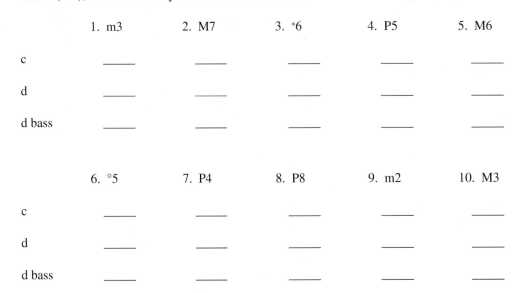

10	11	12	13	14	15	16	17	18	19	20	21	22	23	24

E. Beneath each harmonic interval that follows, indicate whether it is consonant ("c"), dissonant ("d"), or dissonant only if the bass has the bottom note of the interval ("d bass").

	1. m3	2. M7	3. +6	4. P5	5. M6
c	_____	_____	_____	_____	_____
d	_____	_____	_____	_____	_____
d bass	_____	_____	_____	_____	_____

	6. °5	7. P4	8. P8	9. m2	10. M3
c	_____	_____	_____	_____	_____
d	_____	_____	_____	_____	_____
d bass	_____	_____	_____	_____	_____

Chapter 2

ELEMENTS OF RHYTHM

EXERCISE 2–1

A. Show how many notes or rests of the shorter duration would be required to equal the longer duration.

ex. $\textrm{♩} \times \underline{\ 2\ } = \textrm{𝅝}$

1. $\textrm{♩} \times \underline{\quad} = \textrm{𝅗𝅥}$

2. $\textrm{♪} \times \underline{\quad} = \textrm{𝅗𝅥}$

3. $\textrm{♪} \times \underline{\quad} = \textrm{♩ ♪}$

4. $\textrm{𝄾·} \times \underline{\quad} = \textrm{▬·}$

5. $\textrm{𝄿} \times \underline{\quad} = \textrm{▬}$

6. $\textrm{▬} \times \underline{\quad} = \textrm{𝅃}$

7. $\textrm{♩} \times \underline{\quad} = \textrm{𝄶}$

8. $\textrm{♪} \times \underline{\quad} = \textrm{♪·}$

9. $\textrm{♪} \times \underline{\quad} = \textrm{♩·}$

10. $\textrm{♩·} \times \underline{\quad} = \textrm{𝅗𝅥·}$

11. $\textrm{♪} \times \underline{\quad} = \textrm{𝅗𝅥·}$

12. $\textrm{𝄿} \times \underline{\quad} = \textrm{𝄾}$

13. $\textrm{▬·} \times \underline{\quad} = \textrm{▬·}$

14. $\textrm{𝄿} \times \underline{\quad} = \textrm{𝄽·}$

15. $\textrm{♪} \times \underline{\quad} = \textrm{𝅗𝅥··}$

16. $\textrm{♪} \times \underline{\quad} = \textrm{𝅝}$

B. Sing aloud each of the following songs. Then identify the meter type of each, using the terms *duple, triple,* and *quadruple.*

1. "Auld Lang Syne" _____

2. "Star-Spangled Banner" _____

3. "Pop Goes the Weasel" _____

4. "America" ("My Country, 'Tis of Thee") _____

5. "Swing Low, Sweet Chariot" _____

C. Scale review. Fill in the blanks, using the melodic minor for all minor-key examples.

ex. $\hat{6}$ is F♯ in ___*A*___ (M)

1. ↓$\hat{7}$ is C in _____ (m)

2. $\hat{4}$ is _____ in c♯

3. _____ is A in F

4. $\hat{5}$ is C♯ in _____ (m)

5. $\hat{2}$ is _____ in E

6. $\hat{7}$ is A in _____ (M)

7. ↓$\hat{6}$ is _____ in c

8. _____ is C♯ in b

9. $\hat{6}$ is C in _____ (M)

10. _____ is F♯ in g

11. $\hat{4}$ is G in _____ (M)

12. $\hat{5}$ is _____ in G

13. _____ is A♭ in f

14. ↑$\hat{6}$ is C♯ in _____ (m)

EXERCISE 2–2

A. Fill in the blanks.

	Beat and Meter Type	Beat Note	Division of the Beat	Time Signature
1.				𝄴
2.	Simple triple	𝅗𝅥		
3.	Simple duple		♫	
4.		♪		2
5.	Simple quadruple		♫	

B. Renotate the excerpts from textbook Example 2–1 using the specified time signatures.

"Jingle Bells"

"America the Beautiful"

"Home on the Range"

EXERCISE 2-3

A. Fill in the blanks.

	Beat and Meter Type	Beat Note	Division of the Beat	Time Signature
1.	Compound triple	♩.		
2.				6 / 16
3.			♫♪	12
4.	Compound duple		♩ ♩ ♩	
5.		♪.		9

B. Renotate the excerpts from textbook Example 2–2 using the specified time signatures.

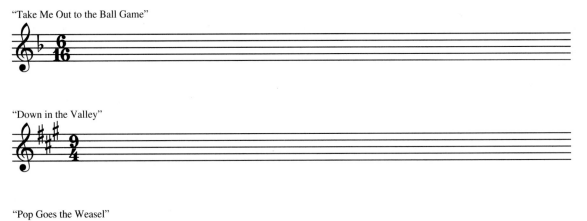

"Take Me Out to the Ball Game"

"Down in the Valley"

"Pop Goes the Weasel"

EXERCISE 2–4

A. Fill in the blanks.

	Beat and Meter Type	Beat Note	Division of the Beat	Time Signature
1.	Compound quadruple		♪♪♪	
2.	Simple triple		♫	
3.			♩ ♩	4
4.		♪.		6
5.				¢
6.			♩ ♩ ♩	9

B. Each measure below is incomplete. Add one or more rests to complete the measure.

C. Provide the best time signature for each measure. In some cases more than one correct answer might be possible.

D. Each of the following fragments is notated so that the placement of the beats is obscured in some fashion. Without changing the way the music will sound, rewrite each one to clarify the beat placement.

E. Add stems as required.

    1. Each duration is a half note.

    2. Each duration is a sixteenth note. Beam them in groups of four.

F. Scale review. Fill in the key, scale degree, or note, whichever is missing. Assume the melodic minor form for all minor keys.

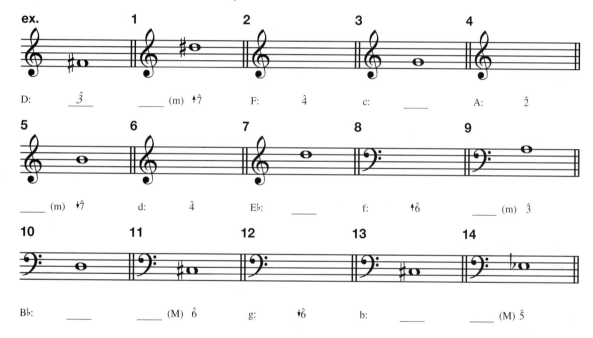

D: $\hat{3}$ ____ (m) ↑$\hat{7}$ F: $\hat{4}$ c: ____   A: $\hat{2}$

____ (m) ↑$\hat{7}$ d: $\hat{4}$ Eb: ____   f: ↑$\hat{6}$ ____ (m) $\hat{3}$

Bb: ____   ____ (M) $\hat{6}$ g: ↑$\hat{6}$ b: ____   ____ (M) $\hat{5}$

G. Interval review. Notate the specified interval above the given note.

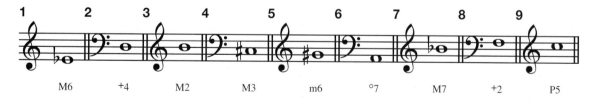

   M6   +4   M2   M3   m6   °7   M7   +2   P5

H. Interval review. Notate the specified interval below the given note.

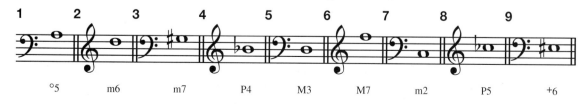

   °5   m6   m7   P4   M3   M7   m2   P5   +6

Chapter 3

INTRODUCTION TO TRIADS AND SEVENTH CHORDS

EXERCISE 3–1

A. Spell the triad, given the root and the type. Major triads are indicated by an uppercase letter (G), minor by an uppercase letter followed by the letter "m" (Gm), augmented by a "+" (G⁺), and diminished by a "°" (G°).

1. Gm _____   **4.** A° _____   **7.** C⁺ _____   **10.** F♯m _____

2. E♭ _____   **5.** Fm _____   **8.** A♯° _____   **11.** B⁺ _____

3. D° _____   **6.** D♭ _____   **9.** E _____   **12.** E♭m _____

B. Fill in the blanks.

	ex.	1	2	3	4	5	6	7	8	9	10
5th:	G♯	A♭	___	F♯	___	___	___	___	___	B	___
3rd:	E	___	___	___	E♭	___	___	B♭	___	A
Root:	C♯	___	D	___	A♭	___	G♯	E♭	___	___	___
Type:	m	M	+	m	m	°	m	M	+	m	°

C. Notate the triad, given the root and the type.

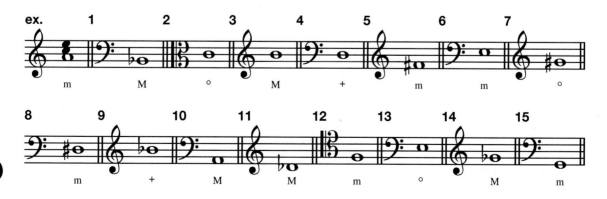

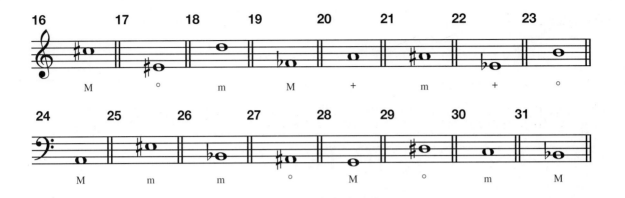

D. Given the chord quality and one member of the triad, notate the remainder of the triad.

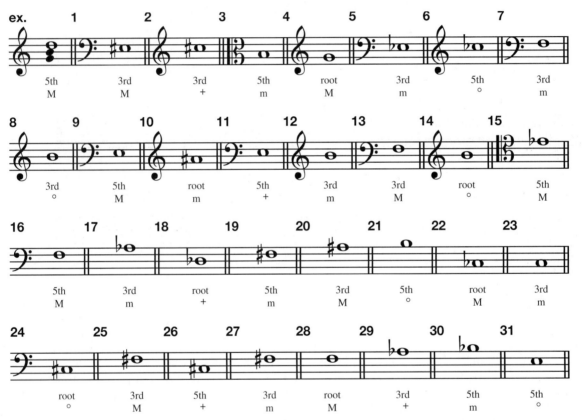

EXERCISE 3-2

A. Identify the type of seventh chord, using the abbreviations given in Example 3–3.

B. Notate the seventh chord, given the root and type.

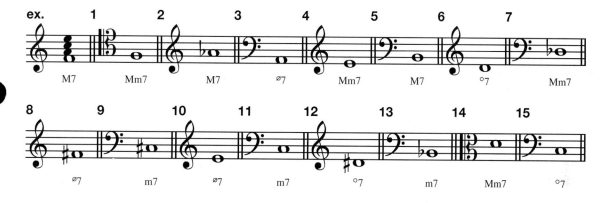

C. Given the seventh-chord quality and one member of the chord, notate the rest of the chord.

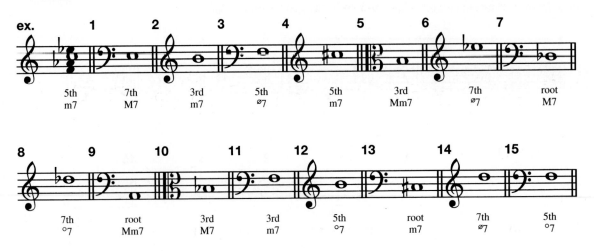

EXERCISE 3–3

A. Identify the root and type of each chord and show the correct bass-position symbol (Bps).

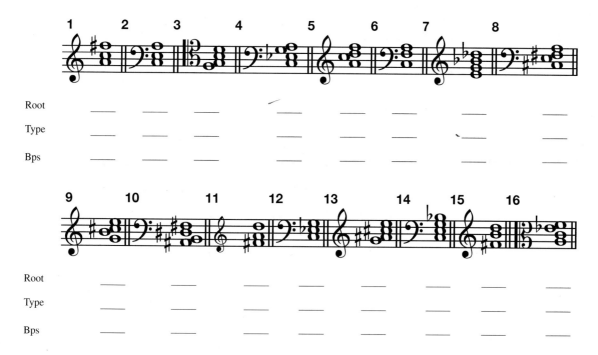

Root ___ ___ ___ ___ ___ ___ ___ ___

Type ___ ___ ___ ___ ___ ___ ___ ___

Bps ___ ___ ___ ___ ___ ___ ___ ___

Root ___ ___ ___ ___ ___ ___ ___ ___

Type ___ ___ ___ ___ ___ ___ ___ ___

Bps ___ ___ ___ ___ ___ ___ ___ ___

B. Fill in the blanks below each figured bass with the lead-sheet symbol of the chord that would be played at the corresponding point in the excerpt by using lead-sheet symbols. The figures 5 and $\frac{5}{3}$ both mean to use a root position triad.

1. Bach, "Gott lebet noch" (adapted)

F	b♭°	C	C♯	F6	g	F6	B♭	F6	B♭	g	C7	F
1	2	3	4	5	6	7	8	9	10	11	12	13

2. Bach, "Dich bet' ich an, mein höchster Gott"

(The first C♯3 in the bass is not to be harmonized.)

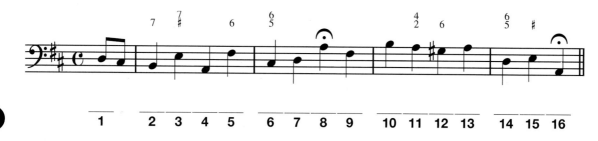

1 2 3 4 5 6 7 8 9 10 11 12 13 14 15 16

3. Corelli, Sonata V, op. 2, Sarabande

C. Notate using half notes on the bottom staff the chords indicated by the lead-sheet symbols. Notate all chords in root position.

Terry, "Serenade to a Bus Seat"

DISK: 1 TRACK: 1

By Clark Terry. © 1958 (renewed 1986) Orpheum Music, Berkeley, CA.

EXERCISE 3–4

A. Label each chord with an appropriate lead-sheet symbol in the space above the chord. You do not need to show bass positions. All the notes in each exercise belong to the same chord.

B. Provide the root, type, and bass-position symbol (Bps) for each chord in the following excerpts. Each chord is numbered. Put your analysis of the chords in the blanks below each excerpt.

1. Bach, "Wer weiss, wie nahe mir mein Ende"

DISK: 1 TRACK: 2

Root _____

Type _____

Bps   **1**   **2**   **3**   **4**   **5**   **6**   **7**   **8**   **9**   **10** **11** **12**   **13** **14**   **15** **16**   **17**

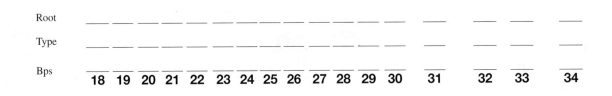

Root _____

Type _____

Bps   **18** **19** **20** **21** **22**   **23** **24** **25** **26**   **27** **28** **29** **30**   **31**   **32** **33**   **34**

2. Schumann, "Ich will meine Seele tauchen," op. 48, no. 5

DISK: 1 TRACK: 3

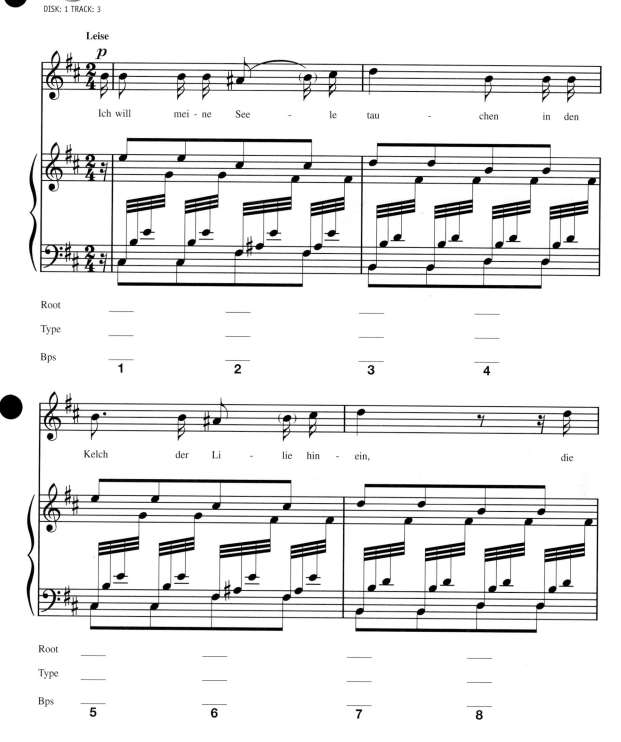

Root ____ ____ ____ ____

Type ____ ____ ____ ____

Bps __9__ __10__ __11__ __12__

Root ____ ____ ____ ____ ____ ____ ____

Type ____ ____ ____ ____ ____ ____ ____

Bps __13__ __14__ __15__ __16__ __17__ __18__ __19__

Name _____ Class _____ Date _____

3. Gottschalk, "Jerusalem"

DISK: 1 TRACK: 4

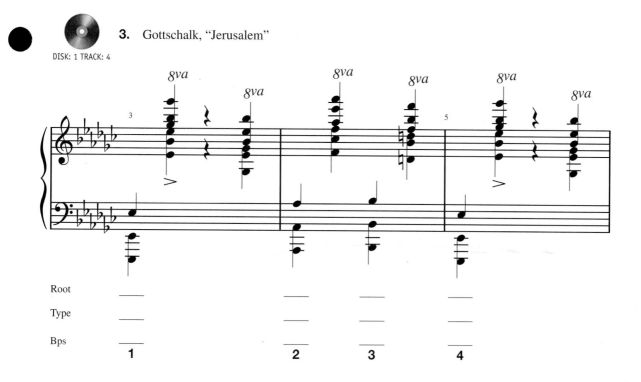

Root ____   ____ ____ ____

Type ____   ____ ____ ____

Bps   **1**   **2**   **3**   **4**

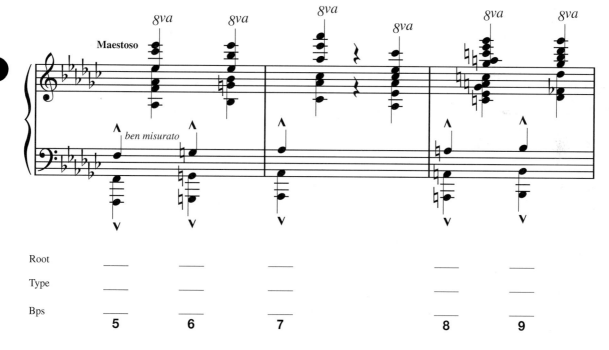

Root ____ ____ ____   ____ ____

Type ____ ____ ____   ____ ____

Bps   **5**   **6**   **7**   **8**   **9**

C. Time signature review. Fill in the blanks.

	Beat and Meter Type	Beat Note	Division of the Beat	Time Signature
1.	Simple triple		♫ (two sixteenth notes)	
2.			♪♪♪ (three eighth notes)	9
3.		𝅗𝅥.		6
4.				4 16

Chapter 4

DIATONIC CHORDS IN MAJOR AND MINOR KEYS

EXERCISE 4–1

A. Given the key and the triad, supply the roman numeral *below* the staff. Be sure your roman numeral is of the correct type (correct case and so on), and include bass-position symbols where needed. Finally, provide an appropriate lead-sheet symbol *above* the staff.

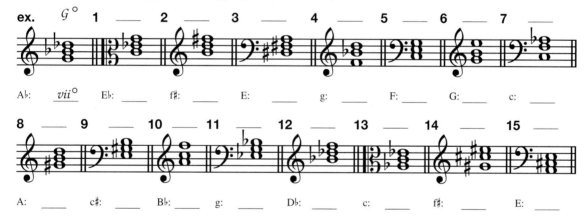

Ab: *vii°*   Eb: ____   f#: ____   E: ____   g: ____   F: ____   G: ____   c: ____

A: ____   c#: ____   Bb: ____   g: ____   Db: ____   c: ____   f#: ____   E: ____

B. In the following exercise you are given the name of a key and a scale degree number (in parentheses). *Without using key signatures*, notate the triad on that scale degree and provide the roman numeral. In minor keys be sure to use the triad types circled in Example 4–7 (p. 63).

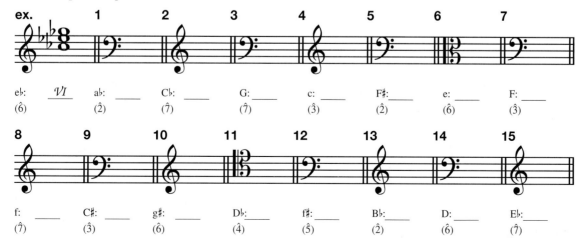

eb: *VI*   ab: ____   Cb: ____   G: ____   c: ____   F#: ____   e: ____   F: ____
(6̂)   (2̂)   (7̂)   (7̂)   (3̂)   (2̂)   (6̂)   (3̂)

f: ____   C#: ____   g#: ____   Db: ____   f#: ____   Bb: ____   D: ____   Eb: ____
(7̂)   (3̂)   (6̂)   (4̂)   (5̂)   (2̂)   (6̂)   (7̂)

31

due monday

C. Analysis. Write roman numerals in the spaces provided, making sure each roman numeral is of the correct type and includes a bass-position symbol if necessary.

1. Handel, "Wenn mein Stündlein vorhanden ist"

DISK: 1 TRACK: 5

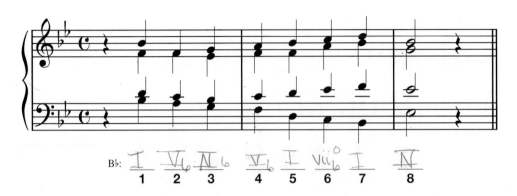

Bb: I   V₆ · IV₆   V₆   I   vii°₆   I   IV
     1   2   3   4   5   6   7   8

2. Handel, "Wenn mein Stündlein vorhanden ist"

DISK: 1 TRACK: 6

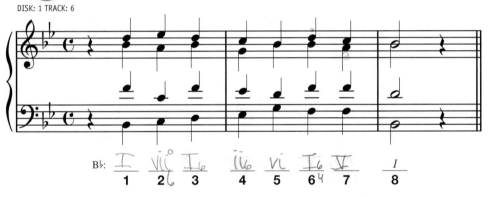

Bb: I   vii°   I₆   ii₆   vi   I₆₄   V   I
     1   2   3   4   5   6   7   8

D. Fill in the blanks, using the example as a model.

	Key	This Chord	Has This Bass Note
ex.	C	I⁶	E
1.	a	V⁶	G#
2.	Eb	IV⁶	C
3.	c#	ii°⁶	F#
4.	B	V⁶₄	C#
5.	g	i⁶₄	D
6.	F	vii°⁶	G

EXERCISE 4–2

A. Given the key and the seventh chord, supply the roman numeral *below* the staff. Be sure your roman numeral is of the correct type, and include bass-position symbols where needed. Finally, provide an appropriate lead-sheet symbol *above* the staff.

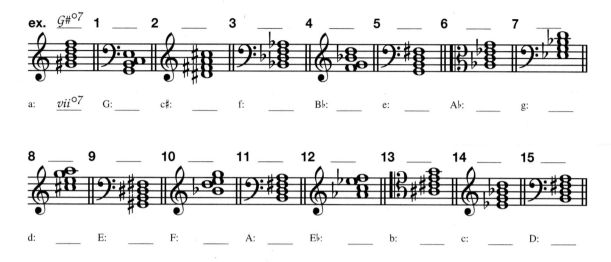

a: *vii°7* G: ____ c♯: ____ f: ____ B♭: ____ e: ____ A♭: ____ g: ____

d: ____ E: ____ F: ____ A: ____ E♭: ____ b: ____ c: ____ D: ____

B. In the following exercises you are given the name of a key and a scale degree number (in parentheses). Without using key signatures, notate the seventh chord on that scale degree in root position and provide the roman numeral. In minor keys, be sure to use the chord types shown in Example 4–9 (p. 67).

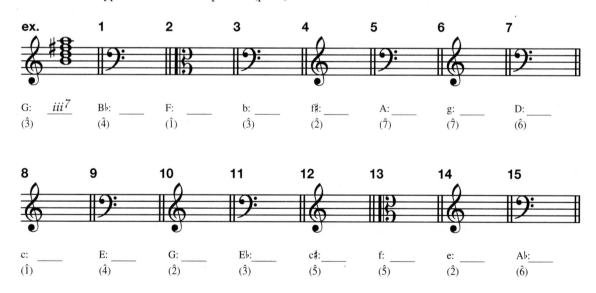

G: *iii7* B♭: ____ F: ____ b: ____ f♯: ____ A: ____ g: ____ D: ____
(3̂) (4̂) (1̂) (3̂) (2̂) (7̂) (7̂) (6̂)

c: ____ E: ____ G: ____ E♭: ____ c♯: ____ f: ____ e: ____ A♭: ____
(1̂) (4̂) (2̂) (3̂) (5̂) (5̂) (2̂) (6̂)

C. Analysis. Put roman numerals in the spaces provided, making sure each roman numeral is of the correct type and includes an inversion symbol, if needed.

DISK: 1 TRACK: 7

1. Beethoven, Nine Variations on a Theme by Paisiello

DISK: 1 TRACK: 8

2. Brahms, "Minnelied," op. 44, no. 1

Chapter 5

PRINCIPLES OF VOICE LEADING

EXERCISE 5–1

A. Criticize each melody in terms of the rules for simple melodies discussed on pages 73–75.

B. Compose simple melodies that will conform to these progressions.

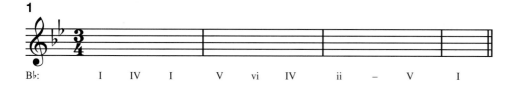

2

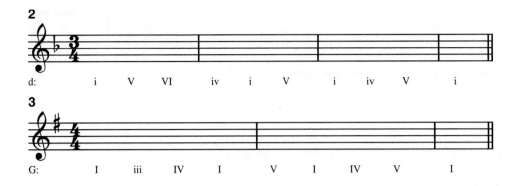

d: i   V   VI   iv   i   V   i   iv   V   i

3

G: I   iii   IV   I   V   I   IV   V   I

EXERCISE 5-2

A. Analyze the following excerpt using roman numerals and bass-position symbols. Then show beneath each roman numeral the structure of the chord by writing "C" or "O" for close or open structure. The notes in parentheses are not part of the chord and should be ignored for the purpose of harmonic analysis.

 Schumann, "Roundelay," op. 68, no. 22

DISK: 1 TRACK: 9

A: ___   ___ ___   ___ ___ ___ V^7 ___

B. Review the two conventions concerning spacing on pages 74–75. Then point out in the following example any places where those conventions are not followed.

C. Fill in the circled missing inner voice(s) to complete each root-position triad, being sure that each note of the triad is represented. Follow the spacing conventions and stay within the range of each vocal part.

D. In the following examples you are given the soprano note for each chord. Supply the alto, tenor, and bass notes to complete the specified triad in close or open position, as indicated. Be sure to double the root of each chord and to follow the spacing conventions.

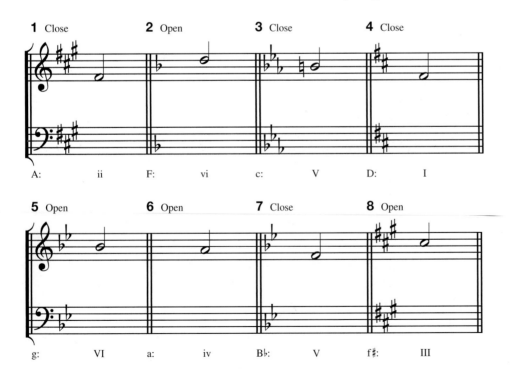

EXERCISE 5–3

A. First, put lead-sheet symbols in the blanks above this example. Then analyze the motion between each of the pairs of voices, and fill in the blanks using this system:

a = static   b = oblique   c = contrary   d = similar   e = parallel

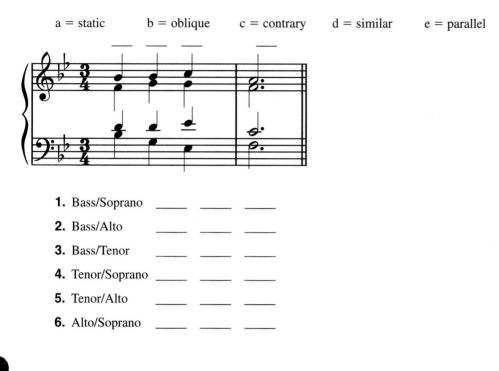

1. Bass/Soprano   ____ ____ ____

2. Bass/Alto   ____ ____ ____

3. Bass/Tenor   ____ ____ ____

4. Tenor/Soprano   ____ ____ ____

5. Tenor/Alto   ____ ____ ____

6. Alto/Soprano   ____ ____ ____

B. Label the chords in the following excerpt with roman numerals. Then label any examples of parallelism (objectionable or otherwise) that you can find.

Bach, "Ermuntre dich, mein schwacher Geist"

DISK: 1 TRACK: 10

C. Find and label the following errors in this passage:

 1. Parallel 8ves

 2. Parallel 5ths

 3. Direct 5th

 4. Consecutive 5ths by contrary motion

 5. Spacing error (review pp. 78–79)

D. Find and label the following errors in this passage:

 1. Parallel 8ves

 2. Parallel 5ths

 3. Direct 8ve

 4. Spacing error

Chapter 6

ROOT-POSITION
PART WRITING

EXERCISE 6–1. *Using repeated triads*

Fill in the inner voice or voices in the second chord of each exercise. The key is F major throughout. Double the roots of the triads in the four-voice examples.

1 four parts

2 three parts

EXERCISE 6–2. *Using roots a 4th (5th) apart*

A. Add alto and tenor parts to each of the following exercises. Each progression involves roots a P4 (P5) apart. Use one of the three methods outlined on pages 91–92 in each case and state which you have used.

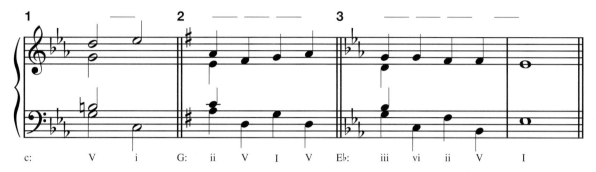

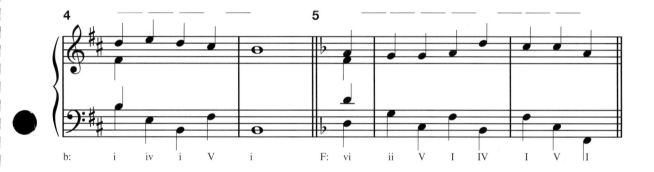

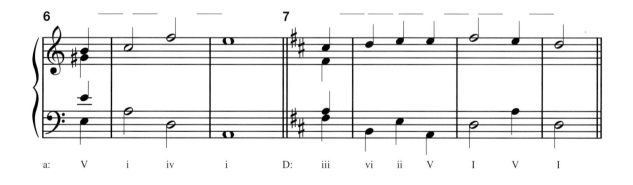

B. Add an alto part to each exercise. Be careful to observe conventions concerning spacing, parallels, and doubling. Each triad should include at least a root and a 3rd.

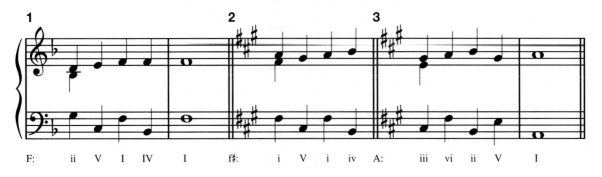

F: ii V   I   IV   I   f#:   i   V   i   iv   A: iii vi ii V   I

EXERCISE 6–3. *Using roots a 4th (5th) and 3rd (6th) apart*

A. Add alto and tenor parts to each exercise that follows. Use the smoothest voice leading in each case. For roots a 4th (5th) apart, state which method you have used.

F: I   vi   IV   ii   g: i   V   i   VI   iv   i   D: I   vi   ii   V   I

E♭:   I   iii   vi   ii   V   I   e: i   VI   iv   i   V   i

B. Add an alto part to each exercise that follows. Be careful to observe the conventions concerning parallels, spacing, and doubling.

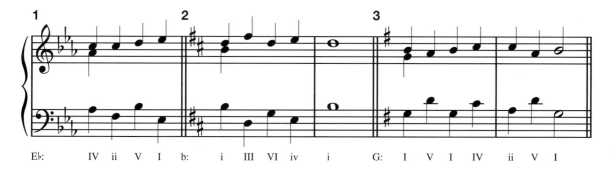

E♭:   IV   ii   V   I   b: i   III   VI   iv   i   G: I   V   I   IV   ii   V   I

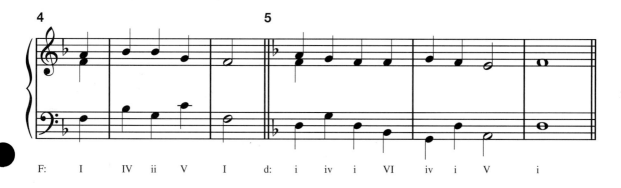

F: I   IV   ii   V   I   d: i   iv   i   VI   iv   i   V   i

EXERCISE 6–4. *Using all root relationships*

A. Complete each progression. Make two versions of each: one for three parts (adding an alto) and one for four parts (adding alto and tenor). In the four-part versions, state which method you have used for any progression by 4th or 5th.

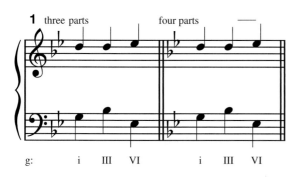

g: i   III   VI   i   III   VI

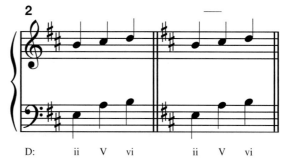

D: ii   V   vi   ii   V   vi

a: iv   V   VI   iv   V   VI

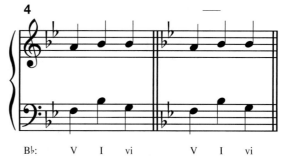

Bb: V   I   vi   V   I   vi

G: I   vi   V   I   vi   V

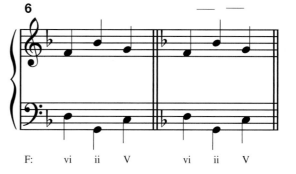

F: vi   ii   V   vi   ii   V

B. Fill in alto and tenor parts in these exercises.

1

A: I vi IV V I IV ii V – I

2

f: i V i VII III iv V – i

3

e: i VII III iv i V VI iv V – i

4

B♭: I – – V I V vi IV V I

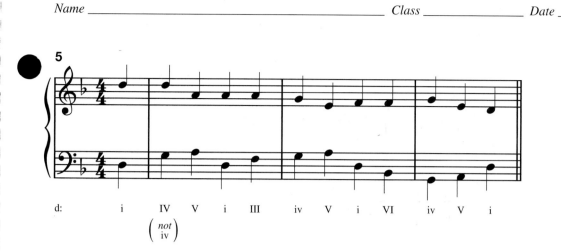

5

d: i   IV   V   i   III   iv   V   i   VI   iv   V   i
         (not)
         (iv)

C. Name the keys and analyze the chords specified by these figured basses. Then compose a good melody line for each. Finally, fill in alto and tenor parts to make a four-part texture.

cl 1
cl 2
HR 1
TbN

b: i   iv   i   III   VI   iv   V   V   i

D. Write the following short progressions in root position for combinations of three and four parts.

1 three parts

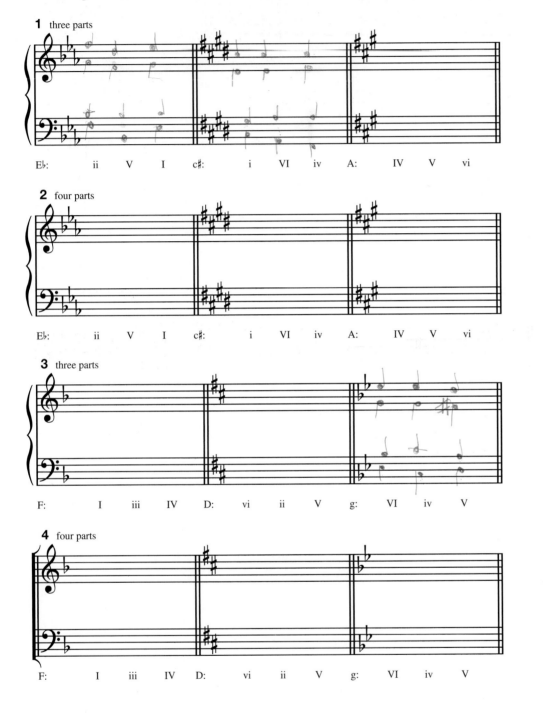

Eb:　　ii　　V　　I　　　c#:　　i　　VI　　iv　　　A:　　IV　　V　　vi

2 four parts

Eb:　　ii　　V　　I　　　c#:　　i　　VI　　iv　　　A:　　IV　　V　　vi

3 three parts

F:　　I　　iii　　IV　　　D:　　vi　　ii　　V　　　g:　　VI　　iv　　V

4 four parts

F:　　I　　iii　　IV　　　D:　　vi　　ii　　V　　　g:　　VI　　iv　　V

EXERCISE 6–5

A. Notate the following chords for the specified instruments. Each chord is written at concert pitch, so transpose as needed for the performers. Use the correct clef for each instrument. Note that the instruments are listed in score order, the order used in Appendix A, which is not always the same as order by pitch.

Fl.	Ob.	Clar. in B♭	Bsn.	A. Sax
T. Sax.	Hn. in F	Tpt. in B♭	Trb.	Hn. in F
Vla.	Vl.	Vc.	D.B.	Tuba

B. Set the following progression for combinations of three and four parts. If possible, score for instruments in your class. Use root position only.

1 three parts (reduced score)

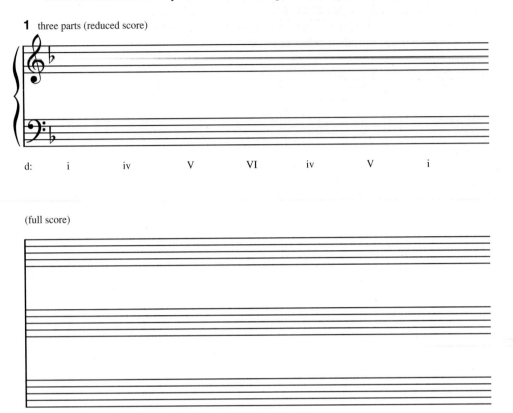

d: i   iv   V   VI   iv   V   i

(full score)

2 four parts (reduced score)

d: i   iv   V   VI   iv   V   i

(full score)

C. Write a version of the following excerpt on a grand staff by transposing the parts to concert pitch. Play your version on the piano and analyze the harmonies if you can.

Chapter 7

HARMONIC PROGRESSION AND THE SEQUENCE

EXERCISE 7–1

A. Complete each harmonic fragment to conform with the major-mode diagram presented on p. 113. The chord in the blank should be different from those on either side of it.

1. IV   __?__   I   (____ or ____)   **4.** iii   __?__   V   (____)

2. vi   __?__   I   (____)   **5.** vii°   __?__   vi   (____)

3. I   __?__   ii   (____ or ____)   **6.** vi   __?__   ii   (____)

B. Bracket any portions of these progressions that do not conform to the chord diagrams on pages 106–113.

1. i   vii°   i   iv   VI   V   i

2. I   vi   ii   IV   I   V   I

3. I   iii   IV   vii°   I   IV   V   I

4. i   III   iv   i   iv   V   vii°   i

C. Analysis. Label all chords with roman numerals and bass-position symbols. Bracket any successions of roman numerals that do not agree with the complete major and minor chord diagrams. In addition, provide lead-sheet symbols above the top staff.

1. Bach, "Du Friedensfürst, Herr Jesu Christ"

DISK: 1 TRACK: 11

DISK: 1 TRACK: 12

2. Vivaldi, Cello Sonata in G Minor, Prelude. Unfigured bass realization by S. Kostka.

Nonchord tones in the solo part have not been put in parentheses, but the harmonic analysis can be done by concentrating on the accompaniment. The key is g minor, despite what appears to be an incorrect key signature. Key signatures had not yet become standardized when this work was composed.

D. Analyze the chords specified by these figured basses and add inner voices to make a
    four-part texture. Bracket all circle-of-fifths progressions, even those that contain only
    two chords. Before beginning, review the part writing for deceptive progressions.

1

2

3

E. Analyze this figured bass, then add a good soprano line and inner voices. Bracket all circle-of-fifths progressions.

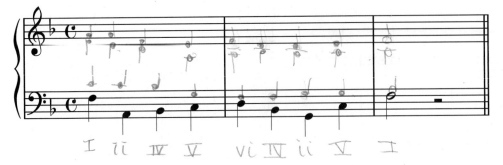

I   ii   IV   V   vi   IV   ii   V   I

F. Add an alto part (only) to mm. 1 and 2. Then compose a good soprano line for mm. 3 and 4 and fill in an alto part.

F: I   V   I   vi   IV   V   I   vi   ii   V   I   V   I

G. Following are two unfigured bass lines. Using triads in root position and first inversion *only,* show a good harmonization of each one by placing roman numerals beneath the bass line. Be sure to refer to the diagrams on p. 113 while you work on your harmonizations.

1

2

H. Harmonize the following melodies by using root-position major or minor (not diminished) triads in an acceptable progression. Try to give the bass a good contour while avoiding parallel and direct 5ths and 8ves with the melody. Be sure to include analysis. Finally, add one or two inner parts to make a version for SAB three-part chorus or SATB four-part chorus, as indicated.

1 SATB

G:

2 SAB

D:
or b:

3 SATB

Eb:

4 SATB

E:

I. Compose a *simple* melody, then follow the instructions for Part H. You might need to revise the melody as you work on the harmonization.

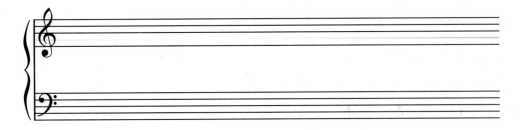

J. Review: Label the chords with roman numerals and bass-position symbols (where needed).

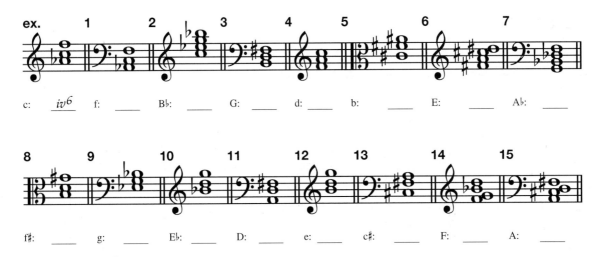

ex.   1   2   3   4   5   6   7

c: *iv⁶*   f: ____   B♭: ____   G: ____   d: ____   b: ____   E: ____   A♭: ____

8   9   10   11   12   13   14   15

f♯: ____   g: ____   E♭: ____   D: ____   e: ____   c♯: ____   F: ____   A: ____

Chapter 8

TRIADS IN FIRST INVERSION

EXERCISE 8–1

A. Analysis.

1. Bracket the longest series of parallel sixth chords (triads in first inversion) that you can find in this excerpt. Do not attempt a roman numeral analysis. Does the voice leading in the sixth-chord passage resemble more closely Example 8–9 (pp. 128–129) or Example 8–10 (p. 129)?

Beethoven, Piano Sonata op. 2, no. 1, III

DISK: 1 TRACK: 13

2. Label all chords with roman numerals. Then classify the doubling in each inverted triad according to the methods shown in Example 8–11 (p. 131).

DISK: 1 TRACK: 14

Bach, "Was frag' ich nach der Welt"

3. Provide lead-sheet symbols (including slash chords) above the excerpt and roman numerals beneath it. Bracket the circle-of-fifths progression (review pp. 104–106).

DISK: 1 TRACK: 15

Handel, Passacaglia

B. The following excerpt is from Mozart's String Quartet K. 428. Supply the missing tenor line (viola in the original).

C. Supply alto and tenor lines for the following passages.

1

g: i⁶ iv⁶ ii°⁶ V A: V I⁶ V⁶ I f: i vii°⁶ i⁶ ii°⁶ V

4   5   6

d: i i⁶ iv i⁶ b: i IV vii°⁶ i E♭: I IV⁶ V⁶ I

7   8   9

E: I vii°⁶ I⁶ ii⁶ G: I V⁶ I I⁶ B♭: I⁶ ii⁶ V I

10   11   12

F: I I⁶ IV V D: I⁶ V⁶ I IV c: i ii°⁶ V VI

D. Supply alto lines for the following passages.

g: i⁶   iv⁶   ii°⁶   V   A: V   I⁶   V⁶   I   f: i   vii°⁶ i⁶   ii°⁶   V

d: i   i⁶   iv   i⁶   b: i   IV   vii°⁶   i   E♭:   I   IV⁶   V⁶   I

E. Analyze the harmonies implied by the following soprano/bass lines and add one or
    two inner parts, as specified by your instructor.

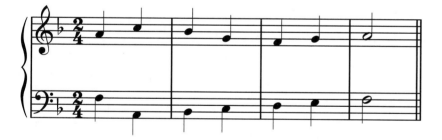

F:

e:

F. The following passage is reduced from Beethoven's Sonata op. 10, no. 3, III. Analyze the implied harmonies (more than one good solution is possible) and add an alto line (only). Use only triads in root position and first inversion.

G. Continue your solution to Part D with a second eight-measure segment. The second part should be similar to the first, but if it starts exactly like it, objectionable parallels will result. Maintain the three-part texture.

H. Review the figured-bass information on pages 47–49. Then realize the figured basses below by following these steps:

    a. Provide the roman numerals specified by the figured bass.

    b. Compose a simple melody that will conform to the progression and at the same time will create a good counterpoint with the bass.

    c. Make two completed versions of each, one for three parts and one for four parts.

1 Three parts

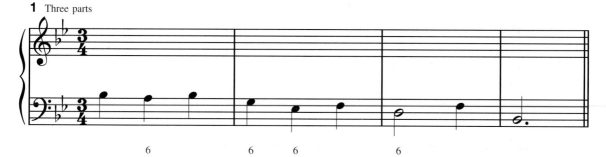

Bb:

Four parts

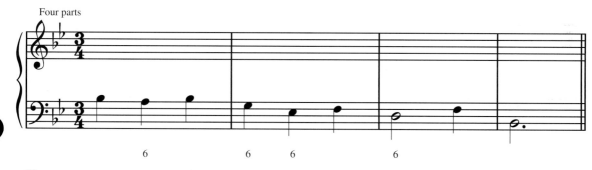

Bb:

2 Three parts (The horizontal line beneath the last measure means that the 3rd above the bass should be retained in the next chord.)

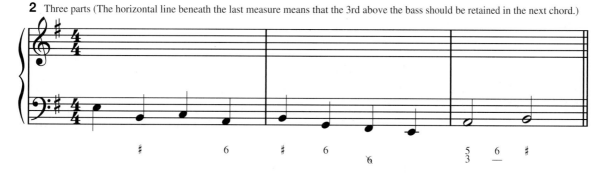

e:

Four parts

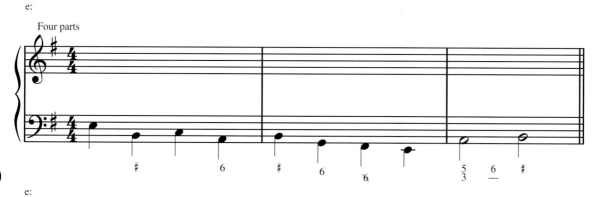

e:

I. Review the chord diagrams on pages 106–113. Then assign roman numerals to each of the bass notes in the following exercises, using triads (only) in root position and first inversion to create a good tonal progression. Then follow steps b and c for Part H. If possible, these settings should be for vocal or instrumental combinations found in your class.

F: I   IV   ii⁰₆   IV₆   V   I   iii   IV   V   I

a:

D:

e: i   VII₆   i₆   ii⁰₆   V   i₆   i   iV   V   V   i

J. Select roman numerals with which to harmonize this melody, changing chords every place there is a blank. Be sure your progression is a good one. Then write out the melody with a bass line, using first-inversion triads where appropriate. Make sure that the bass creates a good counterpoint with the melody and that there are no objectionable parallels. Finally, make a piano setting, using the bass line you composed. Keep the piano texture simple, perhaps like that in Example 8–3 (p. 124).

Chapter 9

TRIADS IN SECOND INVERSION

EXERCISE 9–1

A. Analysis. In addition to the specific instructions for each example, label each six-four chord by type.

  1. Label all chords with roman numerals.

  Schumann, "The Wild Rider," op. 68, no. 8

DISK: 1 TRACK: 16

  2. Label chords with roman numerals.

  Bach, "Nun ruhen all Wälder"

DISK: 1 TRACK: 17

3. Label the chords with roman numerals and put parentheses around all nonchord tones.

Clara Wieck Schumann, Scherzo op. 15, no. 4

DISK: 1 TRACK: 18

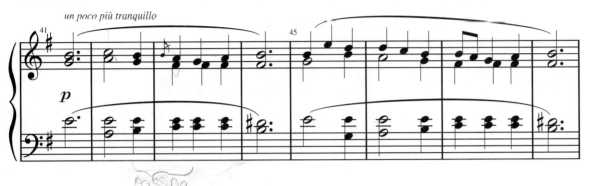

Published 1976 by Willy Müller-Süddeutscher Verlag and 1994 by Breitkopf & Härtel.

4. Label the chords with roman numerals. As before, identify the type of any six-four chord you encounter.

Haydn, Symphony no. 100, I

DISK: 1 TRACK: 19

5. Label the chords with roman numerals, and identify the type of any six-four chords.

Mozart, Piano Sonata K. 331, III

DISK: 1 TRACK: 20

6. Label the chords with roman numerals, and identify the type of any six-four chord you encounter.

Beethoven, Piano Concerto no. 1, op. 15, I

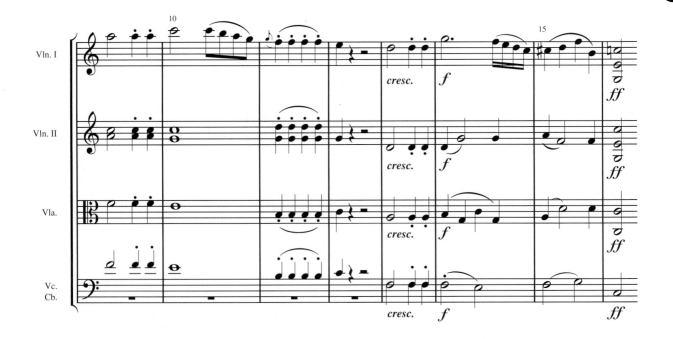

B. Fill in one or two inner parts, as specified. Identify any six-four chords by type.

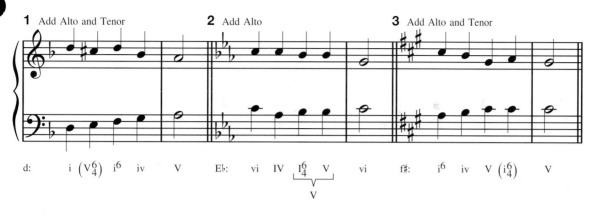

d: i (V⁶₄) i⁶ iv V   E♭: vi IV I⁶₄ V vi   f♯: i⁶ iv V (i⁶₄) V
                                        └─V─┘

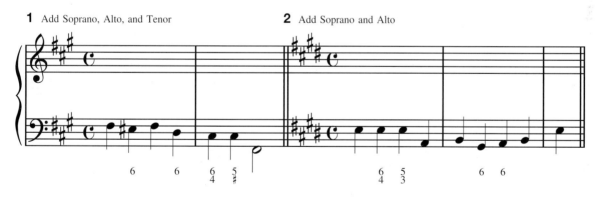

B♭: I (IV⁶₄) I vii°⁶   I⁶ IV V   a: i v⁶ iv⁶ (i⁶₄) ii°⁶ V i

C. Realize these figured basses for three or four voices, as specified, striving to create good outer-voice counterpoint. Notice the frequent use of ⁵₃ (or the equivalent, such as ♯) to indicate root-position triads following an inverted chord. Analyze with roman numerals and label six-four types.

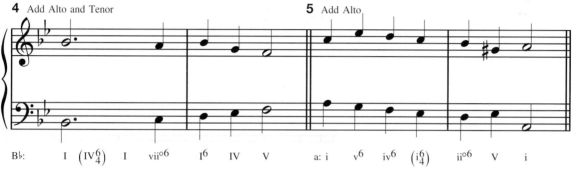

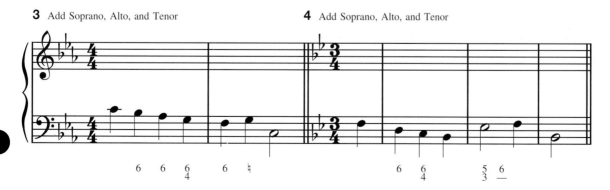

D. Harmonize each unfigured bass with a good tonal progression. Then compose a soprano line that will both fit the progression and create a good outer-voice counterpoint with the bass. Finally, fill in alto and tenor parts to make a four-part texture. Be sure to include a six-four chord in each one and identify the six-four type.

E. Harmonize each melody by composing a bass line that will create a good counterpoint with the melody and that will imply a good harmonic progression. Complete the harmonization by filling in two inner parts. Try to include an appropriate six-four chord in each harmonization.

F.   Continue the accompaniment of this violin melody. Nonchord tones are in parenthe-
     ses. Be sure to use at least one cadential, passing, or pedal six-four chord. Include a
     harmonic analysis.

Bb: I   6

Chapter 10

CADENCES, PHRASES, AND PERIODS

EXERCISE 10–1

A. Cadences. Using only triads in root position and first inversion, compose examples of the following cadences. Each example should include three chords—the two cadence chords plus one chord preceding the cadence chords. Include key signatures and roman numerals.

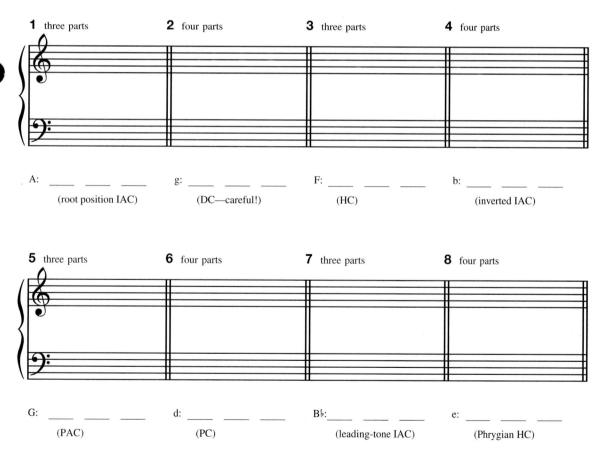

| **1** three parts | **2** four parts | **3** three parts | **4** four parts |

A: ____ ____ ____   g: ____ ____ ____   F: ____ ____ ____   b: ____ ____ ____

(root position IAC)   (DC—careful!)   (HC)   (inverted IAC)

| **5** three parts | **6** four parts | **7** three parts | **8** four parts |

G: ____ ____ ____   d: ____ ____ ____   B♭: ____ ____ ____   e: ____ ____ ____

(PAC)   (PC)   (leading-tone IAC)   (Phrygian HC)

9 three parts   **10** four parts   **11** three parts   **12** four parts

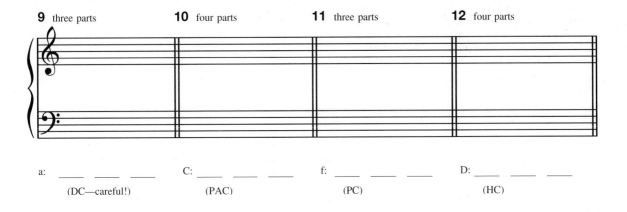

a: ____ ____ ____   C: ____ ____ ____   f: ____ ____ ____   D: ____ ____ ____

    (DC—careful!)   (PAC)   (PC)   (HC)

B. Analysis. The cadence chords have been analyzed for you in each example. Make a diagram of each excerpt similar to the diagrams used in the text. Include phrase labels (a, b, and so on), cadence types and measures, and the form of the example.

1. Each phrase can be analyzed as a sentence. Show x and x' (with brackets) for each phrase in the score.

 Schumann, Symphony no. 1, op. 38, III (piano reduction)

DISK: 1 TRACK: 22

2. Diagram and name the form of this excerpt. Also:

    a. Diagram and name the form of mm. 1–8; then diagram and name the form of mm. 9–16.

    b. Find the best example of imitation between the melody and the bass.

    c. Label the chords implied by the two voices. Nonchord tones are in parentheses in the bass (only). Note: The best choice for m. 5 is *not* a ii chord. (Compare m. 5 with m. 13.)

Anonymous: Minuet in G, from the *Notebook for Anna Magdalena Bach*

DISK: 1 TRACK: 23

[Handwritten annotations: "m1-8 is a sentence: x 1-2, x'-3-4, 4-8"; "a 1-8 HC", "a' 9-16 PAC", "Parallel Period"; "question"; "Half Cad."; chords: "IV I⁶ Plagal C.", "I V", "a'", "PAL", "answer"; "IV I⁶", "V I"]

3. Diagram and name the form of this three-phrase excerpt. How would you explain the descending chords in mm. 3–4 and 7–8?

Haydn, Piano Sonata no. 49, I.

DISK: 1 TRACK: 24

Allegro

[Chords: "IV⁶", "vii°⁶"]

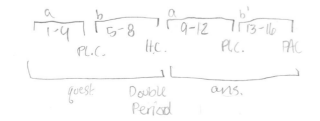

[Handwritten diagram: "a 1-4 b 5-8 a 9-12 b' 13-16", "PL.C. HC. PLC. PAC", "quest. Double Period ans."]

4. Diagram and name the form of this excerpt and copy out any rhythmic motives found in both of the phrases. The progression at *x* resembles an IAC in what key? What is the relationship between that key and e minor?

Mendelssohn, *Song without Words* op. 62, no. 3

DISK: 1 TRACK: 25

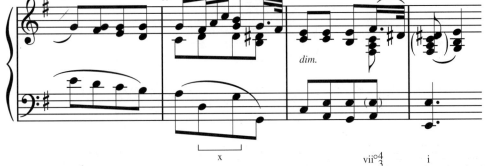

5. This excerpt contains three phrases (some would call it a phrase group). Would it be better to consider it (a) a three-phrase sentence, (b) a period with two antecedent phrases, or (c) a period with two consequent phrases? Why? Which phrase features a circle-of-fifths sequence? Analyze all the chords in that phrase and diagram the form of the excerpt.

Mozart, Piano Sonata K. 545, I

DISK: 1 TRACK: 26

V⁷   I

PAC

6. Diagram the form of this excerpt in four ways, all of which are possible interpretations: (1) all four-measure phrases: 4+4+4+4+4; (2) four phrases, the last one extended: 4+4+4+8; (3) two long phrases plus a short final phrase: 8+8+4; and (4) two phrases, the second extended: 8+12. Which interpretation do you prefer? Why?

 Mozart, Piano Sonata K. 310, III

DISK: 1 TRACK: 27

a: i   V

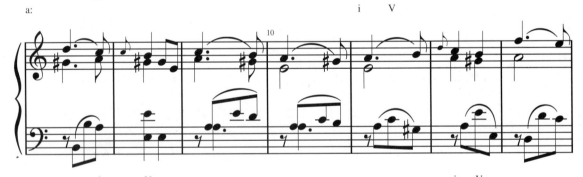

i   V   i   V

V   VI   V   i

f

Name _____ *Class* _____ *Date* _____

7. Diagram and name the form of this theme, then label the first five chords. Also, see if you can find a disguised sequence hidden in the soprano and another in the bass in mm. 1 to 8.

 Beethoven, Piano Sonata op. 13, II

DISK: 1 TRACK: 28

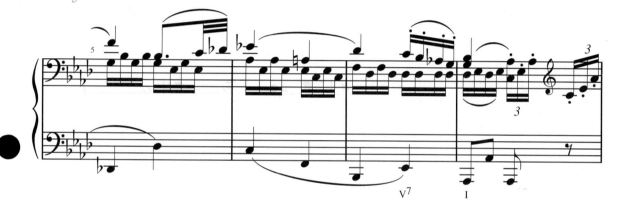

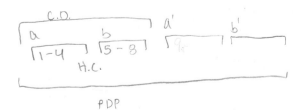

C. Review. Notate the chords in the keys and bass positions indicated.

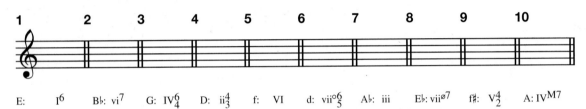

E: I^6 Bb: vi^7 G: IV$^6_4$ D: ii$^4_3$ f: VI d: vii$°^6_5$ Ab: iii Eb: vii^{ø7} f#: V$^4_2$ A: IV^{M7}

Chapter 11

NONCHORD TONES 1

EXERCISE 11–1

A. Analysis.

1. Go back to Example 8-20 (p. 136), which shows NCTs in parentheses, and identify in the following blanks the type of each NCT found in the solo horn part. Always show the interval classification (4–3 and so on) when you analyze suspensions.

m. 6 _____   m. 7 _____ _____   m. 8 _____ _____

m. 10 _____   m. 11 _____ _____

2. Analyze the chords and NCTs in this excerpt. Then make a reduction by (1) removing all NCTs, (2) using longer note values or ties for repeated notes, and (3) transposing parts by a P8 where necessary to make the lines smoother. Study the simplified texture. Do any voice-leading problems appear to have been covered up by the embellishments? Discuss the reasons for the leap in the tenor in m. 3.☐☐☐

Bach, "Hilf, Herr Jesu, lass gelingen"

DISK: 1 TRACK: 29

Reduction

B. After reviewing pages 185–189, decide what *one* suspension would be best in each excerpt that follows. Then renotate with the suspension and at least one other embellishment. Remember to put parentheses around NCTs and to label NCTs and arpeggiations.

C. The following example is a simplified excerpt from a Bach chorale harmonization. Label the chords with roman numerals and activate the texture with stepwise NCTs, including at least one suspension. Label all embellishments.

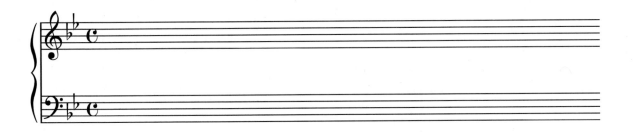

D. In the figured basses that follow, the symbols "4 #" call for a 4–3 suspension, with a sharp applied to the note of resolution. The symbols "6 –" indicate that a first inversion triad is to be used above both Cs in the bass.

For each figured bass, do the following:

1. Analyze the harmonies with roman numerals.

2. Compose a simple but musical soprano line.

3. Fill in one or two inner parts, as specified.

4. Add some stepwise NCTs to each example and label them.

1

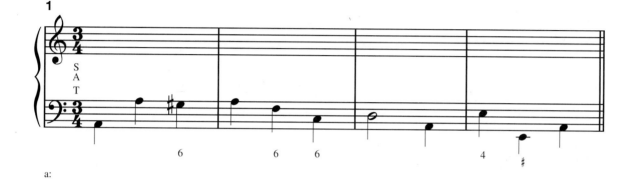

a:

2

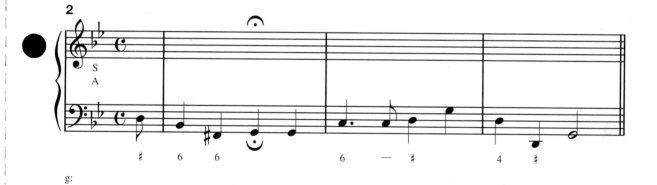

g:

E. Using the following progressions, compose a good soprano/bass framework, using inversions where desired. Next add one or two inner parts, as specified. Show with an *x* every possible location for a 9–8, 7–6, 4–3, or 2–3 suspension. Finally, create an elaborated version of the simple texture, including at least one suspension. Other embellishments should be limited to arpeggiations and stepwise NCTs.

1. Three-part texture. (Remember that diminished triads should be used in first inversion.)

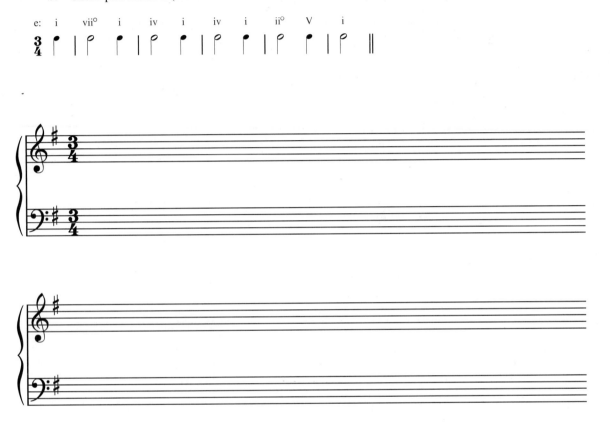

2. Four-part texture.

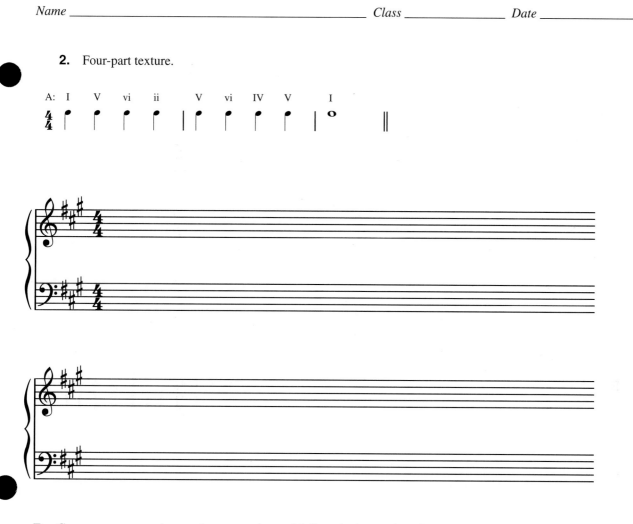

F. Compose your own harmonic progression and follow the instructions for Part E. Try a two-, three-, or four-part texture.

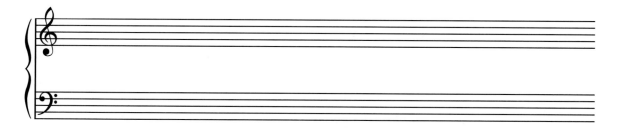

G. Analyze the chords implied by this two-voice framework. Then embellish the frame-
    work in an arrangement for string quartet. A suggested beginning is given.

H. Continue your solution to Part G to form a parallel period.

Chapter 12

NONCHORD TONES 2

EXERCISE 12-1

A. Analysis.

1. Go back to Example 7–17 on page 112 of the text, where NCTs are shown in parentheses, and identify the type of each NCT in the following blanks. Always show the interval classification (7–6 and so on) when you analyze suspensions.

m. 1 _F_   _E_   m. 3 _G#_   _E_

2. Do the same for Example 10–14 on page 166 of the text.

m. 10 _G#_   m. 11 _G_   m. 13 _C_

m. 14 _E_   m. 15 _B_   m. 16, violin: _E_   piano: _C_   _G_

3. Do the same for Example 9–12 on page 150.

VI. I: m. 23 _D_   m. 24 _B_   m. 25 _E_   m. 26 _B_

VI. II: m. 23 _F_   m. 26 _B_   _B_   _B_

4. Label chords and NCTs in this excerpt.

Mozart, Piano Sonata K. 545, II

DISK: 1 TRACK: 30

5. The chords in this excerpt have been labeled for you. Put parentheses around all NCTs in mm. 1 to 6 (only) and label them. The roman numerals in parentheses are part of a "nonfunctional" series of parallel sixth chords (review pp. 128–129), and some other chords have been left unlabeled because they are too advanced for you at this point. The last three measures are included for context, but they are not part of this exercise.

Clara Wieck Schumann, Larghetto, op. 15, no. 1

DISK: 1 TRACK: 31

Published 1976 by Willy Müller-Süddeutscher Verlag and 1994 by Breitkopf & Härtel.

6. NCTs in jazz and popular melodies tend to be used in ways that are not typical of music of earlier centuries. See if you can identify some instances here.

Davis, "Little Willy Leaps"

DISK: 1 TRACK: 32

B. Using a three-part texture, write authentic cadences in five different keys, employing a different NCT from the following list in each cadence: p, n, ant, app, e.

C. Analyze the chords in this phrase with roman numerals. Then renotate the phrase on the following staves, adding at least four NCTs, at least two of which should be suspensions. Label all the NCTs, and show the interval classifications of the suspensions.

D. Compose a simple melody for each figured bass below and fill in inner voices to make a four-part texture. Include some of the NCTs studied in this chapter. Analyze chords and NCTs.

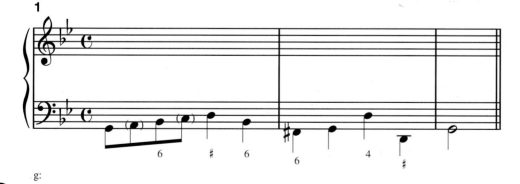

In this example, use a V chord on beat 3 of m. 1. Also, the symbols "6 – –" mean that a first inversion chord is to be maintained throughout m. 2.

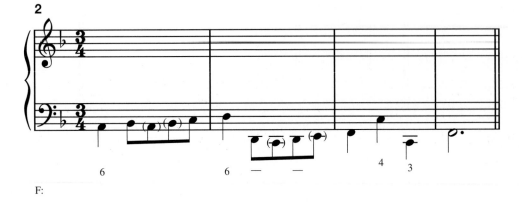

F:

E. Compose a passage in four parts in the key of b minor employing a 7–6 suspension near the beginning and a tonic pedal near the end.

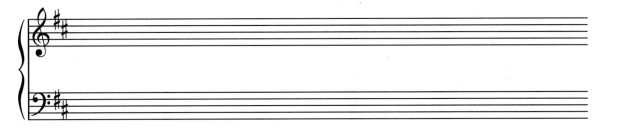

F. Compose eight measures to continue Part A, number 3, on page 72 of this workbook. Maintain a similar texture and end with a PAC. Include an NCT studied in this chapter.

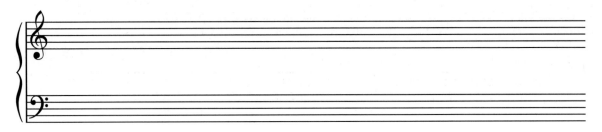

G. The following framework is a simplified version of a passage from Mozart's *Magic Flute*. Embellish the framework, turning it into a vocal part (to be sung on neutral syllables) with piano accompaniment. Try to include at least one chromatic NCT.

H. Continue your solution to Part G to form a parallel period.

Chapter 13

THE V⁷ CHORD

EXERCISE 13–1

A. The note given in each case is the root, 3rd, 5th, or 7th of a V^7 chord. Notate the chord
    in root position and name the major key in which it would be the V^7.

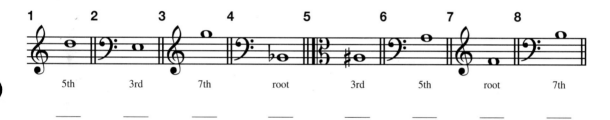

B. Analyze chords and NCTs in the following excerpt, including lead-sheet symbols.
    Then discuss the voice leading in the two V^7 chords. (Note: You might have analyzed
    the Bs in the V chords as passing tones, but consider them to be chord 7ths for the
    purposes of your discussion.)

Bach, "Wir Christenleut'"

DISK: 1 TRACK: 33

C. Resolve each chord to a root position I. (Note: *c* means complete chord, *i* means incomplete chord.)

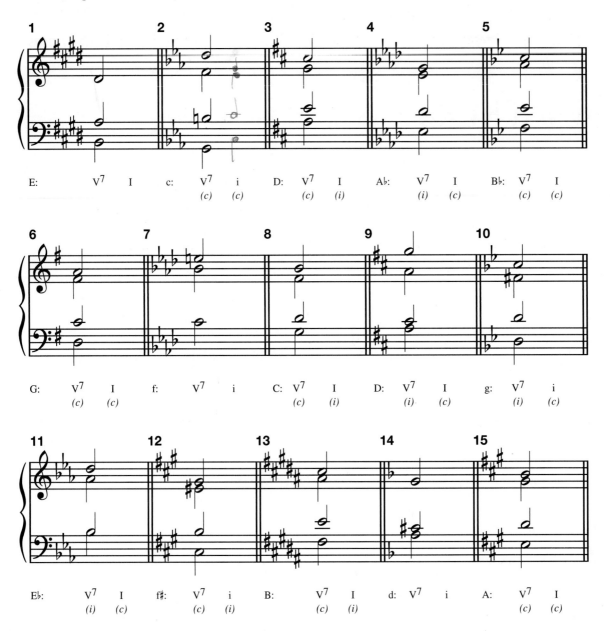

D. Notate the key signature and the V⁷ chord and then resolve it.

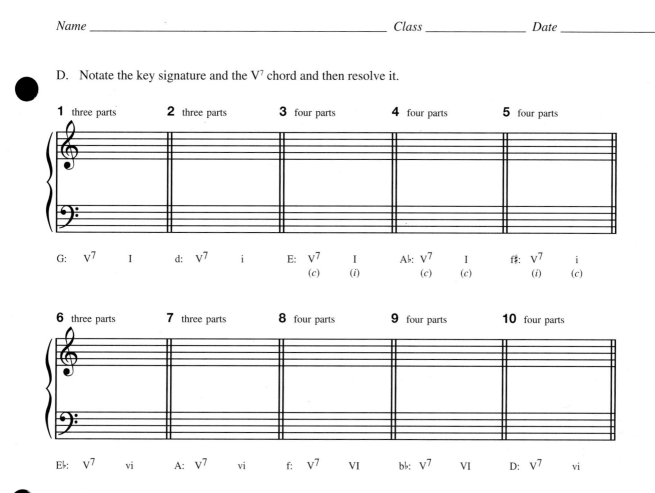

1 three parts   2 three parts   3 four parts   4 four parts   5 four parts

G: V⁷   I   d: V⁷   i   E: V⁷   I   A♭:   V⁷   I   f♯:   V⁷   i
                                          (c)   (i)   (c)   (c)   (i)   (c)

6 three parts   7 three parts   8 four parts   9 four parts   10 four parts

E♭:   V⁷   vi   A: V⁷   vi   f: V⁷   VI   b♭:   V⁷   VI   D: V⁷   vi

E. Analyze the chords specified by this figured bass, using roman numerals and lead-sheet symbols. Then make two harmonizations: one for SAB chorus and one for SATB chorus.

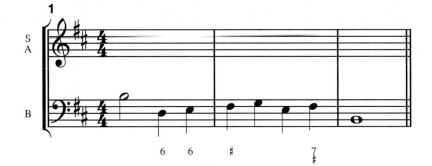

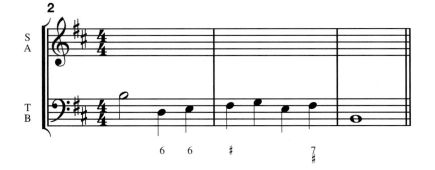

F. Analyze the chords implied by the following soprano and bass lines. Then fill in inner parts. Remember that the tenor part sounds a P8 lower than written.

G. Analyze the harmonies implied by these soprano/bass frameworks. Then make four-
part versions with embellishments and at least one root position V⁷ chord.

1

2

3

H. Set a short text for four-part chorus. The text might be a poem, a headline from a newspaper, or anything. Include at least one V⁷–I progression. Try to keep the motion going through the use of elaborations.

I. Compose a period in a simple three-part texture. End the first phrase with a V⁷–vi DC, the second with a V⁷–I PAC. Then create a version for three instruments, the top part being elaborated by arpeggiations and NCTs, the other two parts in an accompanying role. Turn in both versions.

1. Simple version

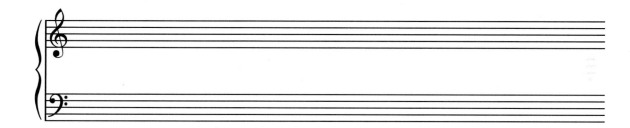

2. Elaborated version

EXERCISE 13–2

A. Notate the specified chords. Use accidentals instead of key signatures.

Db: V_5^6 a: V_3^4 Eb: V_2^4 D: V_3^4 c: V_2^4 F: V_5^6 b: V_2^4 E: V_5^6

B. Label chords and NCTs in the following excerpts. Comment on the treatment of the leading tone and 7th in any V^7 chords in root position or inversion.

Notice that in Exercises 1 and 3, the key signature does not agree with the given key. This is because in each case the music has modulated (changed key) to the dominant. Modulation will be introduced in Chapter 18.

1. Bach, "Ich dank' dir, lieber Herre"

DISK: 1 TRACK: 34

(Which is the more sensible analysis of beat 4 of m. 3: iii_4^6 or V^6?)

F:

2. Beethoven, Piano Sonata op. 2, no. 1, III

DISK: 1 TRACK: 35

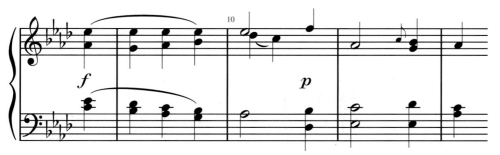

3. Mozart, Quintet for Piano and Winds K. 452, I

DISK: 1 TRACK: 36

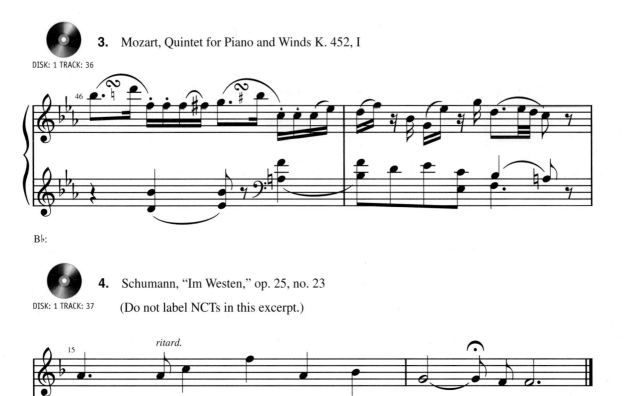

Bb:

4. Schumann, "Im Westen," op. 25, no. 23

DISK: 1 TRACK: 37

(Do not label NCTs in this excerpt.)

mich   und mein   Kind - lein   an's   Herz _____ ged - rückt.

C.   Resolve each chord to a tonic triad (except as indicated). Analyze both chords.

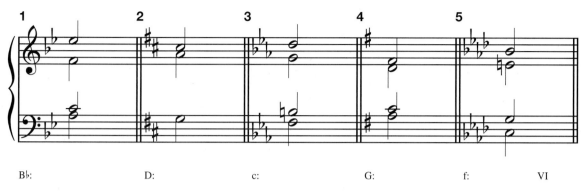

B♭:   D: c: G: f: VI

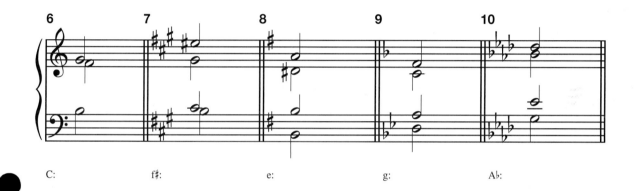

C: f♯:   e: g: A♭:

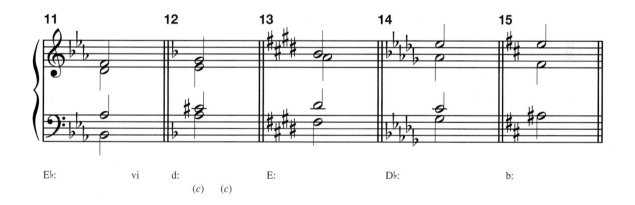

E♭:   vi   d: E: D♭:   b:

                (c) (c)

Name _____ Class _____ Date _____

D. Notate, introduce, and resolve the specified chords. Each chord 7th is to be approached as indicated. Include key signatures, lead-sheet symbols, and roman numerals.

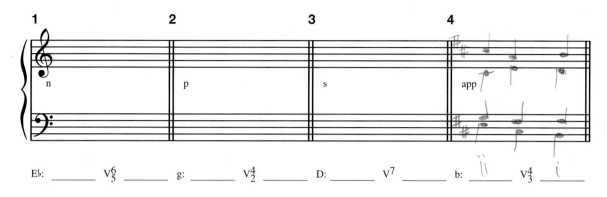

Eb: _____ V^6_5 _____ g: _____ V^4_2 _____ D: _____ V^7 _____ b: ii V^4_3 i

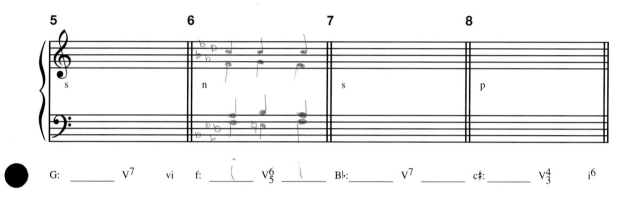

G: _____ V^7 vi f: _____ V^6_5 _____ Bb: _____ V^7 _____ c#: _____ V^4_3 i^6

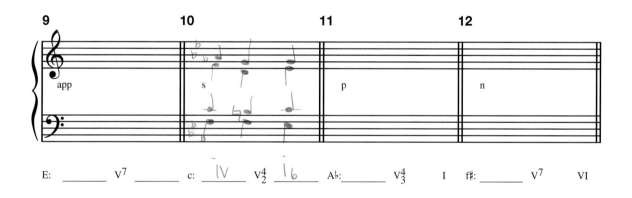

E: _____ V^7 _____ c: IV V^4_2 I^6 Ab: _____ V^4_3 I f#: _____ V^7 VI

E. Show with lead-sheet symbols and roman numerals the chords that this figured bass
   calls for. Then complete the realization in four voices.

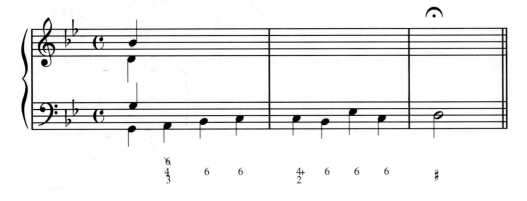

F. Analyze with roman numerals the chords implied by each soprano/bass framework.
    Then add inner parts and embellishments to make a four-part choral texture. Include
    an inverted V⁷ chord.

G. Analyze the chords implied by this soprano/bass framework. Then create a piano texture by filling out some of the chords and adding embellishments. Arpeggiations will be especially useful for prolonging the I chord in mm. 1 and 2. Be sure to include an inverted V^7 chord.

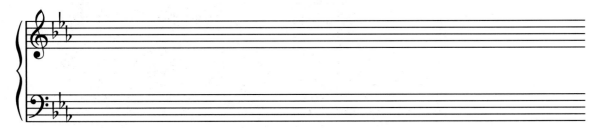

H. Make one or more settings of the following song.

1. Write an arrangement for two B♭ trumpets, unaccompanied. Analyze the harmonies implied by the two lines. Include at least one inverted V^7.

2. Make an arrangement for four-part chorus. Try to elaborate the other voices slightly. Include at least one inverted V^7. Watch out for parallel 8ves and 5ths throughout.

3. Compose a version for piano solo, including at least one inverted V^7. Be prepared to play it, or find someone else in the class who will do so.

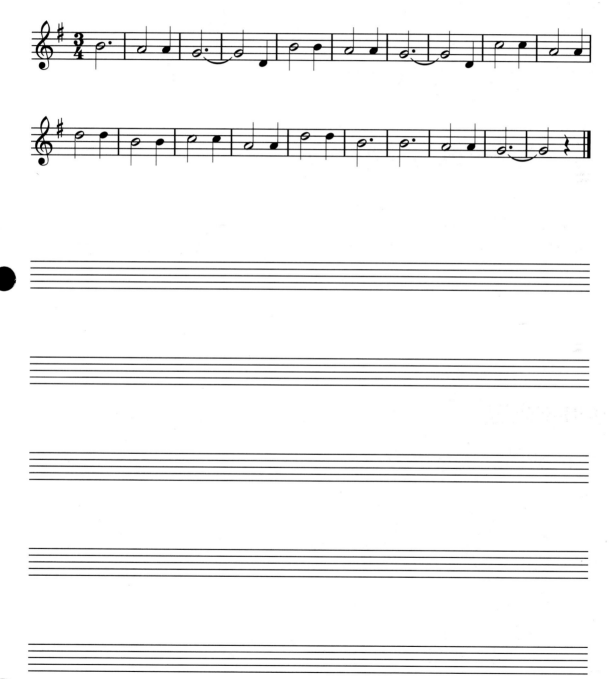

I. Compose a period for a string trio (violin, viola, cello) or for some other combination
    of instruments in your class. Include at least two inverted V^7 chords.

Chapter 14

THE II⁷ AND VII⁷ CHORDS

EXERCISE 14–1

A. Notate the following chords. Use accidentals, not key signatures.

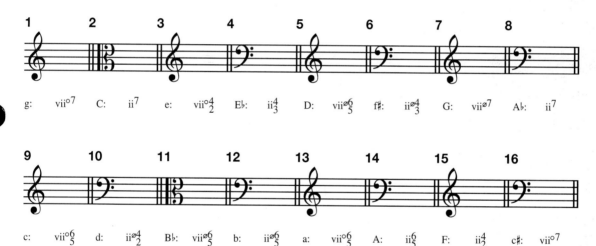

1	2	3	4	5	6	7	8
g: vii°⁷	C: ii⁷	e: vii°⁴₂	E♭: ii⁴₃	D: vii⌀⁶₅	f♯: ii⌀⁴₃	G: vii⌀⁷	A♭: ii⁷

9	10	11	12	13	14	15	16
c: vii°⁶₅	d: ii⌀⁴₂	B♭: vii⌀⁶₅	b: ii⌀⁶₅	a: vii°⁶₅	A: ii⁶₅	F: ii⁴₂	c♯: vii°⁷

B. Analyze the following chords. Be sure your symbols indicate chord quality and inversion.

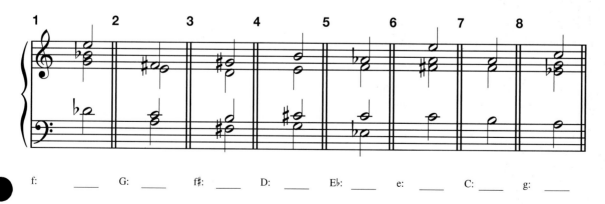

f: _____   G: _____   f♯: _____   D: _____   E♭: _____   e: _____   C: _____   g: _____

C. Analyze the chords and NCTs in the following excerpts. Whenever a ii^7 (ii$^{\emptyset7}$) or vii$^{\emptyset7}$ (vii$^{\circ7}$) chord in root position or inverted is encountered, discuss the voice leading into and out of the chord.

1. Bach, "Jesu, der du meine Seele"

DISK: 1 TRACK: 38

2. Bach, "Herzliebster Jesu, was hast du verbrochen"

DISK: 1 TRACK: 39

b:

3. Bach, *Well-Tempered Clavier,* Book I, Prelude I

DISK: 1 TRACK: 40

C:

4. Label the chords in the blanks provided. Do not label NCTs in this excerpt. The *m.v.* dynamic markings stand for *mezza voce*, "half voice," which means approximately the same thing as *mezzo forte*, or *mf*. The tempo is *Poco Adagio*.

Haydn, String Quartet op. 50, no. 6, II

DISK: 1 TRACK: 41

5. Label the chords and NCTs in this excerpt. These are the third and fourth phrases of the double period that makes up the opening theme. Although too long to be quoted here, the entire theme (mm. 1–30) is worth studying.

Haydn, String Quartet op. 20, no. 4, I

D. Notate, introduce, and resolve the specified chords. Approach each chord 7th as a suspension, a neighbor, or a passing tone, as specified. Include key signatures, lead-sheet symbols, and roman numerals.

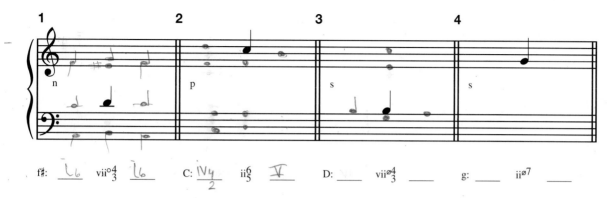

f#: ___ i6   vii°4/3   i6   C: IV4/2   ii6/5   V   D: ___   vii∅4/3   ___   g: ___   ii∅7   ___

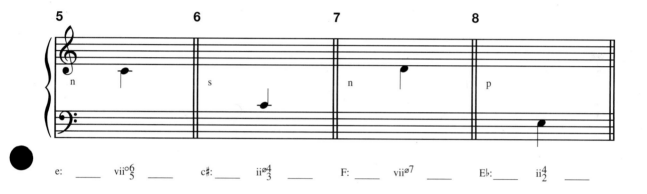

e: ___   vii°6/5   ___   c#: ___   ii∅4/3   ___   F: ___   vii∅7   ___   E♭: ___   ii4/2   ___

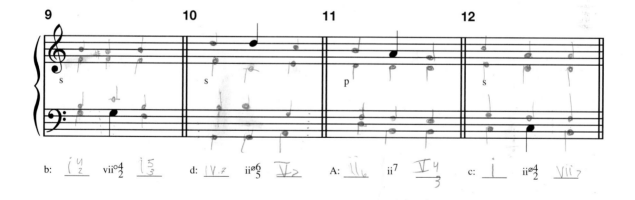

b: i4/2   vii°4/2   i5/3   d: IV.7   ii∅6/5   V2   A: ii6   ii7   V4/3   c: i   ii∅4/2   VII7

E. Analyze these figured basses and continue the realizations, keeping the keyboard
    texture but following conventional part-writing procedures.

1.

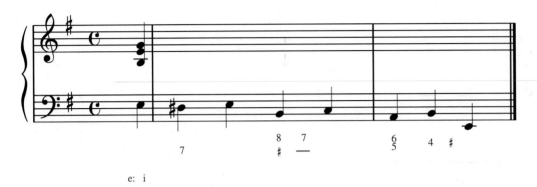

e: i

2. Bach, St. Matthew Passion, no. 20

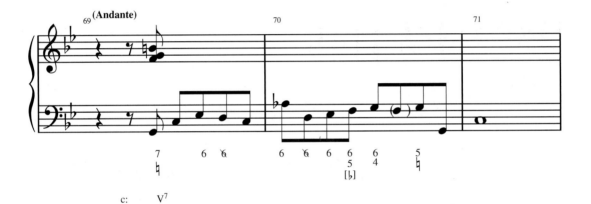

c: V⁷

F.   Harmonize these chorale phrases for four-part chorus.

1. Include a root position ii^7.

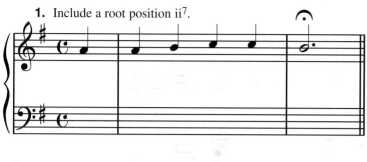

G:

2. Include a root position vii^{o7} and a 4–3 suspension.

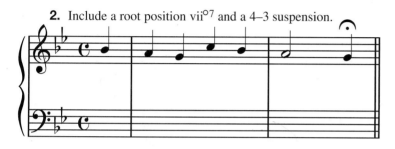

g:

3. Include a ii$^{\varnothing 4}_{2}$ and a deceptive cadence. Some eighth-note chords will be necessary.

d:

4. Include a vii$^{\varnothing 4}_{3}$ and a passing tone.

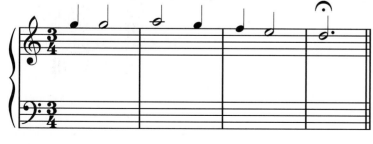

C:

G. Make a setting of the folk song below for some combination of voices and/or instruments available in your class. Include one of the chords discussed in this chapter.

Chapter 15

OTHER DIATONIC SEVENTH CHORDS

EXERCISE 15-1

A. Notate the following chords. Use accidentals, not key signatures.

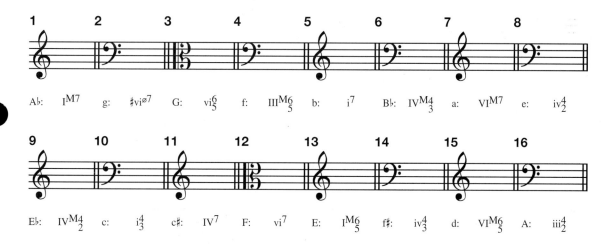

B. Analyze the following chords. Be sure your symbols indicate chord quality and inversion.

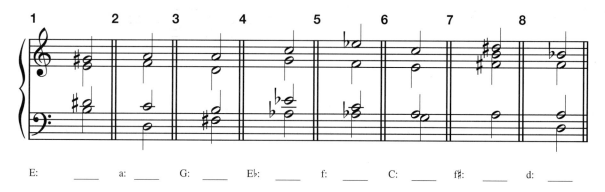

C. Analyze the chords in the following excerpts. Comment on the voice leading involving any of the chords discussed in this chapter.

1. Chopin, Mazurka in a minor, op. posth.

2. Bach, "Herr Jesu Christ, du höchstes Gut"

3. Corelli, Concerto Grosso op. 6, no. 1, VII

D: iii

DISK: 1 TRACK: 46

4. Haydn, Piano Sonata no. 30, I

After you finish labeling all the chords, complete the three-part reduction of mm. 86–92 that follows the excerpt. The neighbor figures in 16th notes in mm. 84–91 are NCTs, not the sevenths of chords.

f♯:

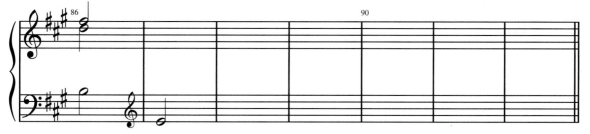

Textural reduction

D. Continue this four-part elaboration of Example 15–18 (p. 251).

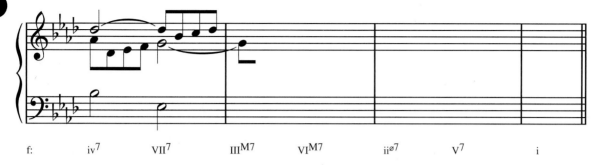

f: iv⁷ VII⁷ III^M7 VI^M7 ii°⁷ V⁷ i

E. Notate, introduce, and resolve the specified chords. Approach each chord 7th as a suspension, a neighbor, or a passing tone, as specified. Include key signatures, lead-sheet symbols, and roman numerals.

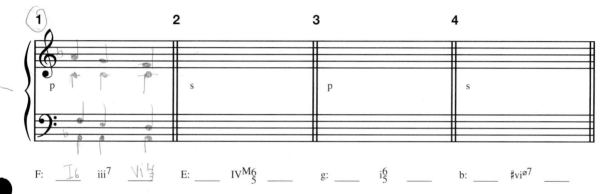

1 2 3 4

F: I6 iii⁷ VI 4/3 E: ____ IV^M6/5 ____ g: ____ i6/5 ____ b: ____ ♯vi°⁷ ____

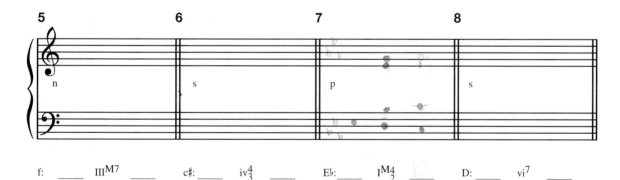

5 6 7 8

f: ____ III^M7 ____ c♯: ____ iv4/3 ____ E♭: ____ I^M4/2 ____ D: ____ vi⁷ ____

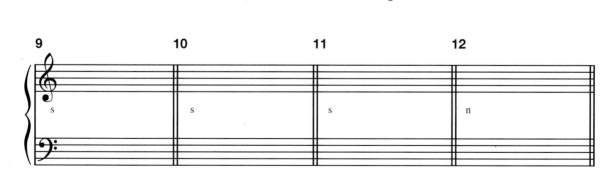

9 10 11 12

s s s n

G: ___ 6/5 IV^M4/2 ___ 6/5 c: ___ 7 VI^M4/3 ___ 7 B♭: ___ 7 I^M7 ___ 7 d: ___ IV6/5 ___

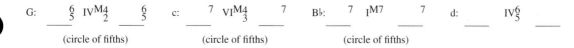

(circle of fifths) (circle of fifths) (circle of fifths)

F. Analyze the chords called for by the figured bass that follows. Remember that the figured-bass symbols are part of the music, not part of the harmonic analysis, which should be written beneath it. Then continue the four-part realization of that figured bass. Note: Be sure to review pages 191–192 before proceeding. (Figures in the fifth measure added by the authors.)

  Corelli, Concerto Grosso op. 6, no. 12, V

DISK: 1 TRACK: 47

G. Analyze this figured bass and continue the realization, keeping the keyboard texture but following conventional part-writing procedures.

Corelli, Concerto Grosso, op. 6 no. 9, "Preludio"

F: I

H. Compose a passage for three voices or instruments containing a sequence of seventh chords similar to that used in the excerpt of Part F.

I. The following is a simple note-against-note contrapuntal framework. Analyze the implied harmonies, then elaborate it into a passage containing several seventh chords. Use four parts or a free keyboard texture. Your final version might be complex, but the original framework should be retained. Include roman numerals and NCT analysis.

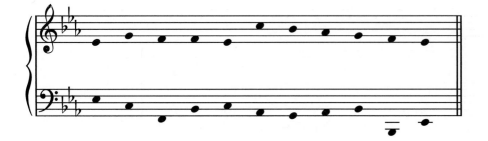

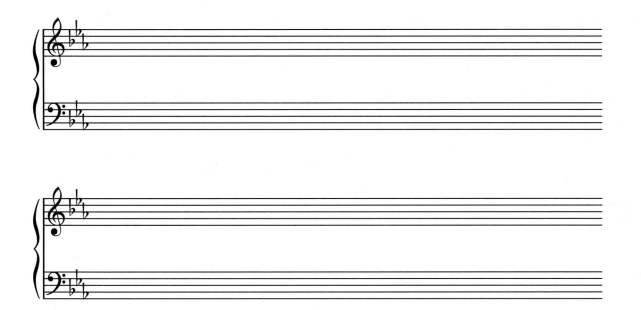

J.   Create a framework similar to Exercise I but in the minor mode. Be sure that it implies a good harmonic progression. Then create an elaboration that employs some of the seventh chords discussed in this chapter. If possible, score for a combination of instruments in your class.

Chapter 16

SECONDARY FUNCTIONS 1

EXERCISE 16–1

A. Review the material on spelling secondary dominants (p. 262). Then notate these secondary dominants in the specified inversions. Include key signatures and lead-sheet symbols.

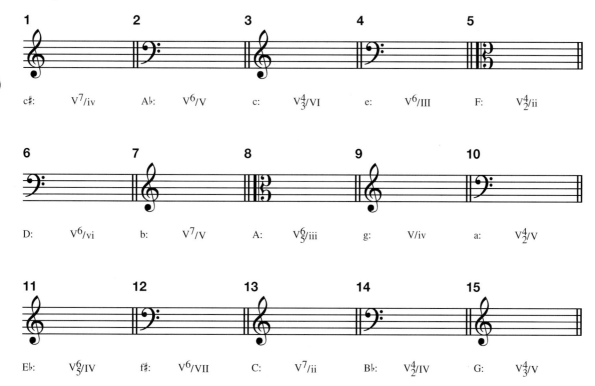

1. c#: V^7/iv
2. A♭: V^6/V
3. c: V^4_3/VI
4. e: V^6/III
5. F: V^4_2/ii

6. D: V^6/vi
7. b: V^7/V
8. A: V^6_5/iii
9. g: V/iv
10. a: V^4_2/V

11. E♭: V^6_5/IV
12. f#: V^6/VII
13. C: V^7/ii
14. B♭: V^4_2/IV
15. G: V^4_3/V

B. Label any chord that might be a secondary dominant according to the steps outlined on
   pages 262–263. Label all others with an *x*.

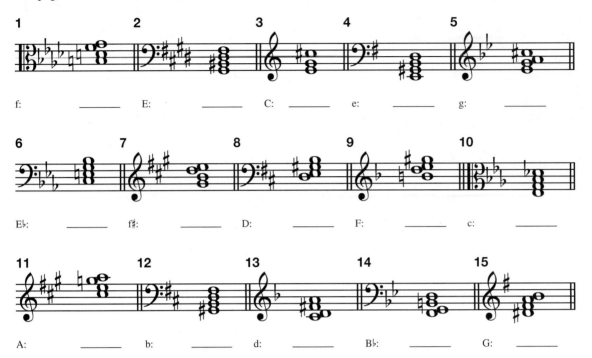

f: _____   E: _____   C: _____   e: _____   g: _____

Eb: _____   f#: _____   D: _____   F: _____   c: _____

A: _____   b: _____   d: _____   Bb: _____   G: _____

Name _____ Class _____ Date _____

EXERCISE 16–2

A. Analysis.

1. Label chords and NCTs. Identify any six-four chords by type. This excerpt contains a set of parallel 5ths in a context that Bach must have found acceptable because he used them so often in this situation. See if you can find them.

 Bach, "Freuet euch, ihr Christen alle"

DISK: 1 TRACK: 48

f:

2. Label the chords with roman numerals. Thinking in terms of chord roots, find the longest harmonic sequence in this excerpt.

Beethoven, Piano Sonata op. 2, no. 1, I

DISK: 1 TRACK: 49

3. Analyze with roman numerals the chords called for by these lead-sheet symbols, referring to Appendix B if necessary. Then continue the accompaniment, keeping the four-part texture and using conventional voice leading. It may be helpful to review Example 16–7 before you begin.

 Fields and Kern, "Pick Yourself Up"

DISK: 1 TRACK: 50

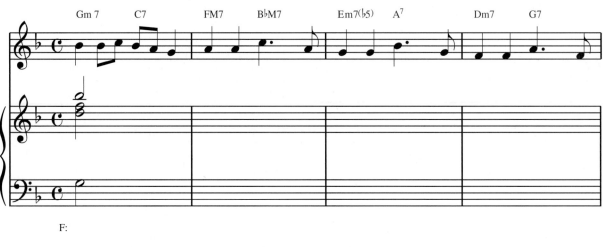

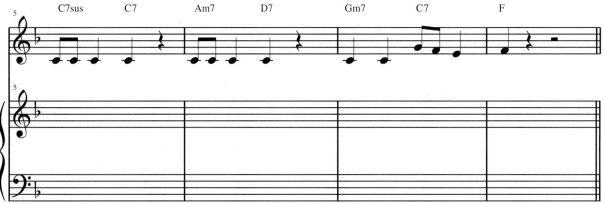

4. Label chords and NCTs. Ignore the grace notes in your harmonic and NCT analysis; for example, the E♭5 in m. 1 is an upper neighbor ornamented by the appoggiatura grace note. Comment on Chopin's use of F♯ and F♮ in this excerpt. Where do they occur? Are they ever in conflict? The form of the excerpt is a (parallel/contrasting) (period/double period).

Chopin, Mazurka op. 67, no. 2

DISK: 1 TRACK: 51

5. Label chords and NCTs. What is the form of this excerpt? (Note: Measures 1–2 are introductory.)

 Beethoven, String Quartet op. 135, III

DISK: 1 TRACK: 52

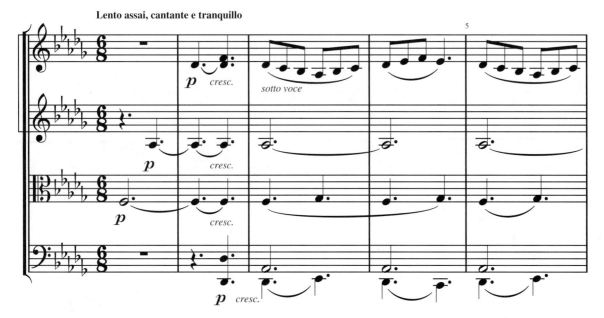

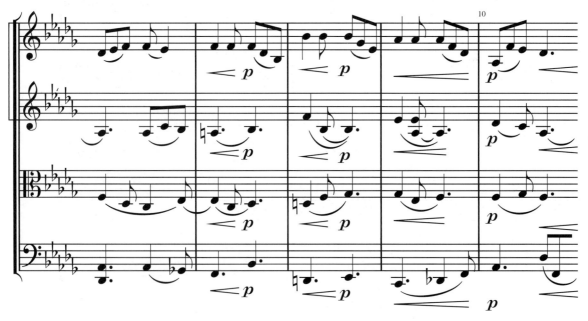

6. Label the chords with roman numerals. Label NCTs in the solo bassoon part only. The
note under the fermata in m. 49 represents a V chord. It was at this point that the soloist
improvised a cadenza. The conductor waited until he heard the soloist arrive at the G3
(often trilled), at which point he would signal the orchestra to be ready for its entrance
in m. 50.

Mozart, Bassoon Concerto K. 191, II

DISK: 1 TRACK: 53

B. For each of the following problems, first analyze the given chord. Next, find a smooth
way to lead into the chord. Although there are many possibilities, it will often work to
use a chord whose root is a P5 above the root of the secondary dominant. Experiment
with other relationships also. Then resolve each chord properly, taking special care
with the leading tone and 7th resolutions. Analyze all chords.

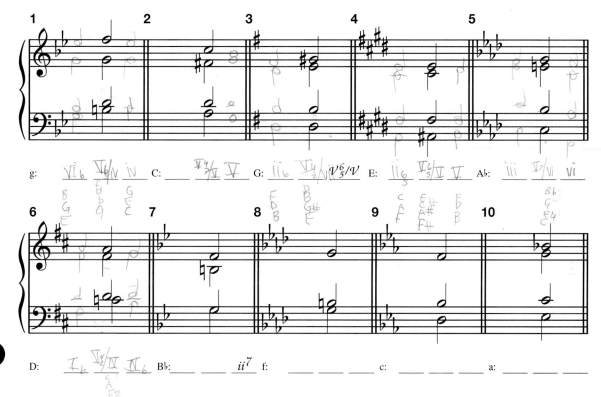

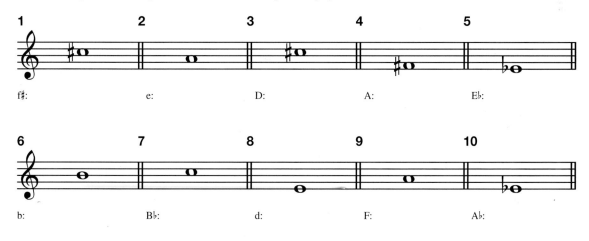

C. List below each note the secondary V and V⁷ chords that could harmonize that note.
You might find it helpful to refer to the examples on page 261.

D. Provide roman numerals to show how the first note could be harmonized as a secondary dominant. The second note should be harmonized by the tonicized chord.

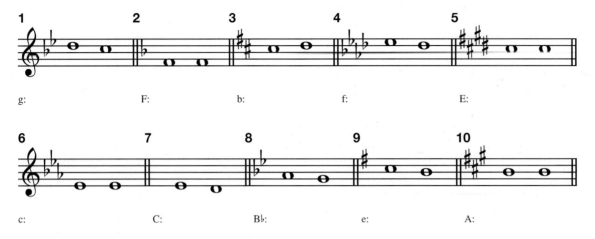

g: F: b: f: E:

c: C: B♭:   e: A:

E. Analyze the chords specified by each figured bass, then make an arrangement for SATB chorus. Strive for smooth voice leading, even if this results in a dull soprano line.

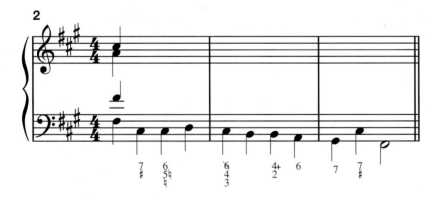

F. Harmonize each chorale phrase for SATB chorus. Include one or more secondary dominants in each phrase and activate the texture with some NCTs.

1

E♭:

2

d:

3

C:

4

g:

G. Analyze the harmonies implied by the following soprano/bass framework. Then make a more interesting version for piano, beginning with the two measures given in the example that follows.

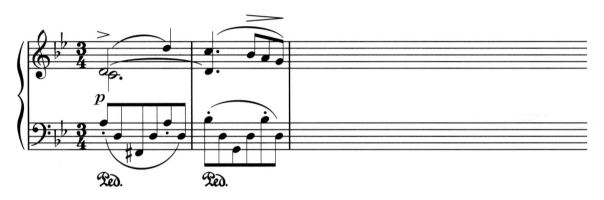

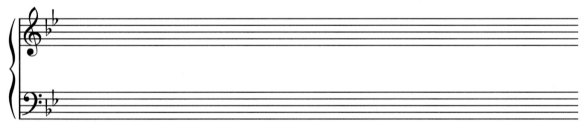

H. Continue the following example to make a total of at least eight measures. Include one or more secondary dominants and end with a PAC. Then score it for four instruments found in your class. Analyze all chords and NCTs.

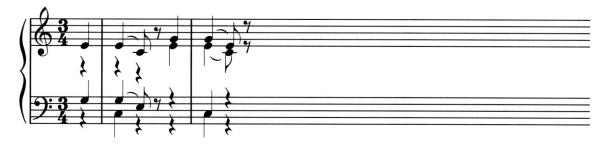

I. Finish the analysis of the following phrase. This phrase is to serve as the *a* phrase of a longer theme you will compose. The theme will be in the form of a parallel double period. Include at least one secondary dominant.

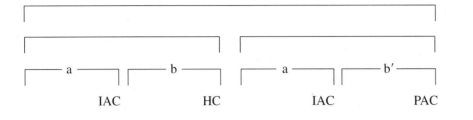

a | b | a | b'

IAC   HC   IAC   PAC

A: (I)   (V⁷)   I

A: (I) (V^7) I

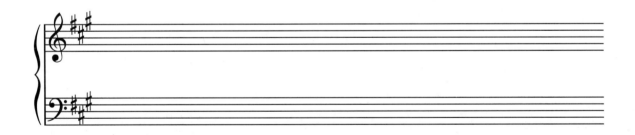

Chapter 17

SECONDARY FUNCTIONS 2

EXERCISE 17–1

A. Review how to spell secondary leading-tone chords (pp. 278–279). Then notate these
    secondary leading-tone chords in the specified inversion. Include key signatures.

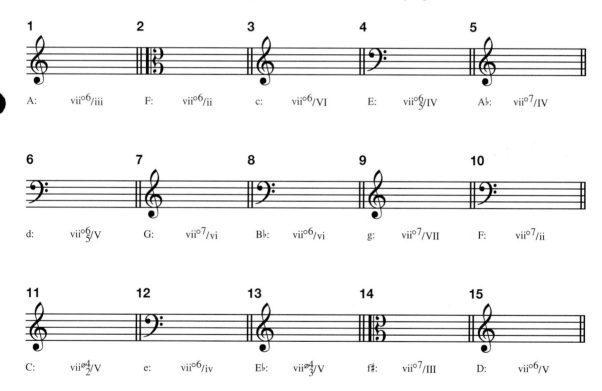

1	2	3	4	5
A: vii°6/iii	F: vii°6/ii	c: vii°6/VI	E: vii°6/5/IV	A♭: vii°7/IV

6	7	8	9	10
d: vii°6/5/V	G: vii°7/vi	B♭: vii°6/vi	g: vii°7/VII	F: vii°7/ii

11	12	13	14	15
C: vii∅4/2/V	e: vii°6/iv	E♭: vii∅4/3/V	f#: vii°7/III	D: vii°6/V

B.   Label any chord that would be a secondary leading-tone chord according to the steps outlined on page 279. Label all others with an *x*.

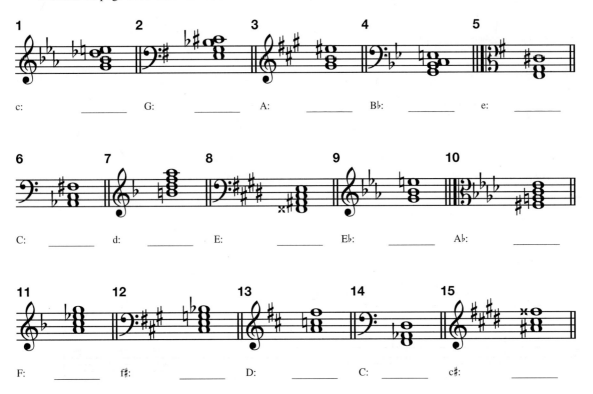

1. c: _____ 2. G: _____ 3. A: _____ 4. Bb: _____ 5. e: _____

6. C: _____ 7. d: _____ 8. E: _____ 9. Eb: _____ 10. Ab: _____

11. F: _____ 12. f#: _____ 13. D: _____ 14. C: _____ 15. c#: _____

EXERCISE 17-2

A. Analysis.

1. In the brilliant and witty concluding passage that follows, Mozart combines the antecedent and consequent phrases from the beginning of the minuet (marked *a* and *b* in mm. 55–58).

   a. Mark all occurrences of *a* and *b*.

   b. Find where the *b* phrase is used in imitation.

   c. Find inverted (upside down) statements of *a* and *b*.

   d. Find a place where original and inverted statements of *b* occur simultaneously.

   e. Put roman numerals in the blanks provided. NCTs are in parentheses.

 Mozart, String Quartet K. 464, II

DISK: 1 TRACK: 54

6   7   8 I_4^6

9

10 11   12   13   14   15

2. Label the chords with roman numerals (the Italian augmented sixth chord in m. 4 will be discussed in Chapter 23). Use your imagination and your ear in analyzing the last chord in m. 2.

Schumann, "Die Löwenbraut," op. 31, no. 1

DISK: 1 TRACK: 55

3. Label chords and NCTs. (An optional piano accompaniment is omitted from the example.) What is the form of this excerpt?

Brahms, "Und gehst du über den Kirchhof," op. 44

DISK: 1 TRACK: 56

4. Analyze chords and NCTs. Find two circle-of-fifths progressions that contain more than four chords. What is the form of this excerpt?

Tchaikovsky, "Morning Prayer," op. 39, no. 1

DISK: 1 TRACK: 57

5. This short song is given here in its entirety. Analyze the chords and NCTs. There are some places where alternative analyses are possible—in m. 1, for example, where the line G♯–F♯–E could be analyzed as chord tones or as passing tones. Think of two analyses for the second chord in m. 11, one of them being a secondary function.

Schumann, "Aus meinen Thränen spriessen," op. 48, no. 2

DISK: 1 TRACK: 58

B. For each of these problems, first analyze and resolve the given chord, being especially careful with the chord 7th and the leading tone. Then find a smooth way to lead into the given chord. Analyze all chords with roman numerals and lead-sheet symbols.

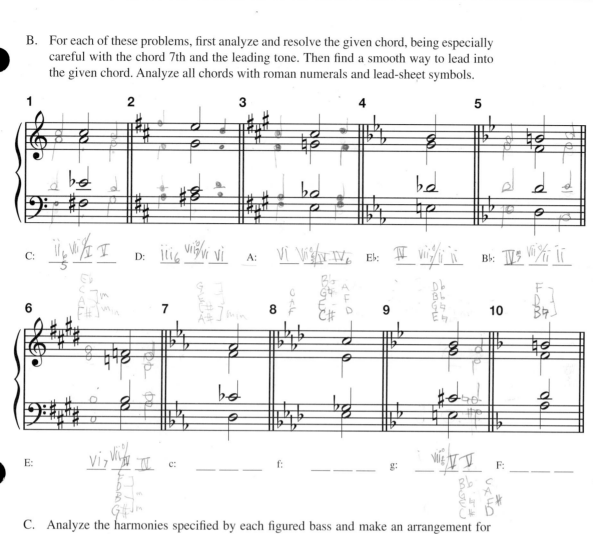

C: $\text{ii}^{\flat}_{5}$ $\text{vii}^{\varnothing}/\text{I}$ I   D: ii^{6}_{6} $\text{vii}^{\varnothing}/\text{vi}$ vi   A: VI $\text{vii}^{\varnothing}_{3}/\text{IV}$ $\text{IV}_{\flat}$ E♭: IV $\text{vii}^{\varnothing}_{7}/\text{ii}$ ii   B♭: IV^{m}_{7} $\text{vii}^{\varnothing}/\text{ii}$ ii

E: VI_{7} $\text{vii}^{\varnothing}/\text{IV}$ IV   c: ___ ___ ___   f: ___ ___ ___   g: $\text{vii}^{\varnothing}_{6}/\text{V}$ V   F: ___ ___ ___

C. Analyze the harmonies specified by each figured bass and make an arrangement for SATB chorus. Try to use smooth voice leading, even at the expense of an interesting soprano line.

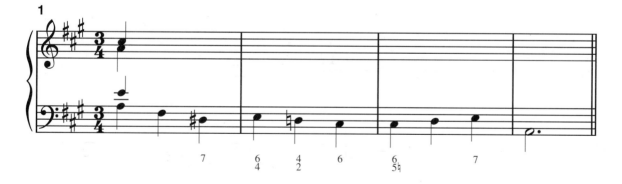

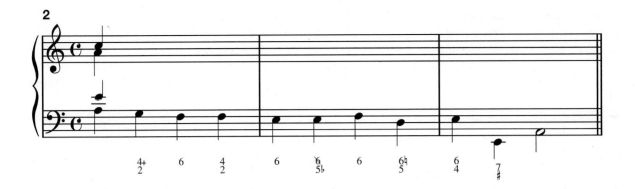

D. Harmonize each of these chorale phrases for SATB chorus. Include at least one secondary leading-tone chord or incorporate some other aspect discussed in this chapter in each harmonization.

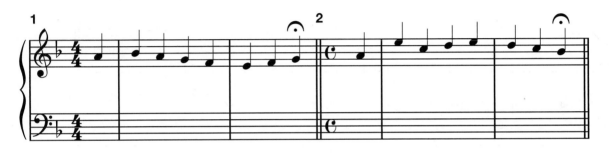

F: a:

F:

E. Each item that follows contains two versions of the same excerpt, one of them in a simple texture and one more elaborate. Continue the simple texture first, including some aspect of harmony discussed in this chapter. Then continue the elaboration, using your simple version as a framework. Label chords and NCTs.

1a.

1b.

2a.

2b.

F. Below is the harmonic progression from "St. Thomas," a jazz standard by Sonny
    Rollins. (Other versions of the progression also exist, which is not uncommon for jazz
    tunes.) Continue the piano accompaniment using conventional voice leading. As a
    bonus, listen to the Sonny Rollins performance (Prestige B000FIHBDG) and notate
    the melody on the top staff.

Chapter 18

MODULATIONS USING DIATONIC COMMON CHORDS

EXERCISE 18-1

A. Name the relative key in each case.

1. G♭ _____   6. d _____
2. A _____   7. F♯ _____
3. e _____   8. c♯ _____
4. g _____   9. A♭ _____
5. C♯ _____   10. a♭ _____

B. Name all the keys closely related to the given key. Be sure to use uppercase for major, lowercase for minor.

1. b _____ _____ _____ _____ _____

2. e♭ _____ _____ _____ _____ _____

3. G _____ _____ _____ _____ _____

4. B _____ _____ _____ _____ _____

5. F _____ _____ _____ _____ _____

6. f♯ _____ _____ _____ _____ _____

C. Name the relationship in each case (enharmonically equivalent, parallel, relative and closely related, closely related, foreign).

1. D/e _____   6. A♭/C♭ _____
2. e♭/G♭ _____   7. C♯/D♭ _____
3. A/a _____   8. g♯/c♯ _____
4. d♯/G _____   9. a♭/b♭ _____
5. B♭/F _____   10. c/E♭ _____

EXERCISE 18-2

A. Analysis.

1. This excerpt modulates from B♭ to F, its dominant. The blanks beneath the music show where the bass changes but do not indicate the location of the common chord. NCTs in mm. 1 and 8 (only) have been identified for you. Begin by supplying lead-sheet symbols, and then provide the roman numerals.

Szymanowska, Nocturne

DISK: 1 TRACK: 59

2. Label chords and NCTs in this chorale, which is presented in its entirety. Which two phrases are very similar melodically? What portion of these phrases is harmonized similarly? What chord is emphasized in the first half of the second of these two phrases?

Bach, "Uns ist ein Kindlein heut' geborn"

DISK: 1 TRACK: 60

Tonal Harmony

3. This example, also a complete chorale, is in g minor, although it ends with a major triad (the "Picardy third"). Label chords, but not the NCTs. Notice how often the melody follows an arch contour (inverted in the second phrase). Bracket those arch contours in the melody. If you find any similar contours in the bass, bracket them also.

 Bach, "Jesu, der du meine Seele"

DISK: 1 TRACK: 61

4. Label the chords with roman numerals. How do the pickup notes at the beginning of the excerpt help smooth the return to the first key when the repeat is taken?

 Mozart, Piano Sonata K. 330, II

DISK: 1 TRACK: 62

5. Label the chords with roman numerals.

 Fanny Mendelssohn Hensel, "Das Meer erglänzte weit hinaus."

DISK: 1 TRACK: 63

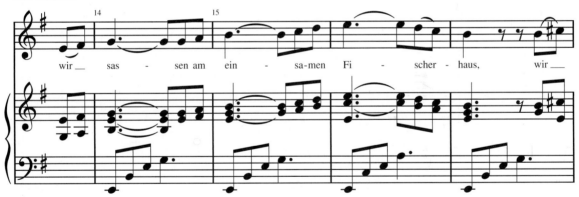

6. Listen to this song all the way through. Then list every tonality that is touched on in the song, either by simple tonicization or by modulation. Which (other than tonic) is referred to again at the end of the song? Decide on one or two tonalities (other than tonic) that represent modulations rather than tonicizations. Then label all chords with roman numerals.

Schumann, "Wenn ich in deine Augen seh'," op. 48, no. 4

DISK: 1 TRACK: 64

Wenn ich in dei - ne Au - gen seh', so schwin-det all' mein Leid und Weh; doch

wenn ich küs - se dei - nen Mund, so werd' ich ganz und gar ge - sund. Wenn

ich mich lehn' an dei - ne Brust, kommt's ü - ber mich wie Him - mels - lust;   doch wenn du

sprichst: Ich lie - be dich,   so muss ich   wei-nen bit - ter - lich.

7. This excerpt begins in A♭ and ends in g minor, modulating through yet another key in the process. Label all chords, and label the NCTs in the vocal part. The German augmented sixth chord in m. 49 will be discussed in a later chapter.

Mozart, Marriage of Figaro, K. 492, "Voi che sapete"

DISK: 1 TRACK: 65

8. Label the chords with roman numerals. In an Alberti bass accompaniment, such as the left hand in this example, the bass note for each chord is usually considered to be the lowest note struck. So in m. 9 the only *bass* notes are D and C♯.

Beethoven, Piano Sonata op. 10, no. 3, II

DISK: 1 TRACK: 66

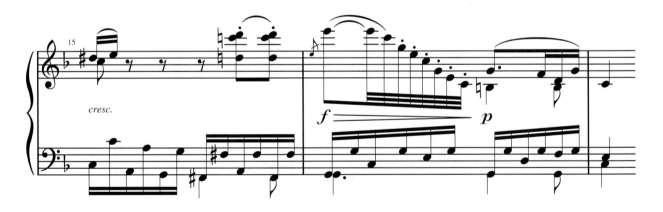

F

B. Fill in the name of the new key on the second line of each exercise.

1. e: i   ii°⁶   V$_2^4$ i⁶   iv⁶

⎿ _a_ :   i⁶   V$_2^4$ i⁶   ii°⁶   V⁷   i

2. D: I   V   I⁶   vii°⁶

⎿ _b_ :   ii°⁶   i$_4^6$ V   i

V

3. F: I   vii°⁶   I⁶   vi

⎿ _c_ :   ii   vii°⁶   I   V$_5^6$ I

4 part
Write

4. g: i   V$_5^6$ V$_2^4$/iv   iv6   V   i⁶

⎿ _d_ :   iv⁶   ii°⁶   V⁷   i

5. b: i   ii$_2^{ø4}$ V$_5^6$ i   VI   iv⁶

⎿ _D_ :   ii⁶   I$_4^6$ V⁷   I

V

6. E♭:   I   ii⁶   V   vi

⎿ _g_ :   iv   ii$_5^{ø6}$ V   VI   iv   V   i

7. A: I   V$_3^4$ I⁶   V⁶

⎿ _b_ :   IV⁶   V$_5^6$ i   ii$_5^{ø6}$ i$_4^6$ V⁷   i

V

8. c: i   V⁷   VI   iv

⎿ _A_ :   vi   IV⁶   (I$_4^6$)   ii$_5^6$ V   I

C. List the diatonic triads that could serve as common chords between each pair of keys. In minor keys, assume the usual chord qualities: i, ii°, III, iv, V, VI, vii°.

ex. First key, C: I   iii   V   vi
Triads: C   Em   G   Am
Second key, G: IV   vi   I   ii

1. First key, E:
Triads:
Second key, f♯:

2. First key, D♭:
Triads:
Second key, G♭:

3. First key, c:
Triads:
Second key, B♭:

4. First key, f:
Triads:
Second key, A♭:

5. First key, B:
Triads:
Second key, F♯:

6. First key, A♭:
Triads:
Second key, B♭:

D. Choose two of the progressions from Part B. Arrange one for SATB chorus and the other for SAB chorus. Activate the texture with NCTs and/or arpeggiations. Arrange the metric and rhythmic structure so that the last chord comes on a strong beat. Label chords and NCTs.

E.   Harmonize the following chorale tunes for SATB chorus.

    1.   In the first phrase, modulate from i to III. The second phrase should return to i.

    2.   Modulate from I to vi in phrase 1. Return to I in phrase 2.

F.   Analyze the chords specified by this figured bass and then make an arrangement for
    SATB chorus.

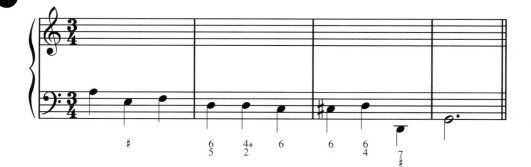

G. Continue this soprano/bass framework, analyzing the implied harmonies. Phrase 1 (mm. 1–4) should end with a HC in f. Phrase 2 (mm. 5–8) should end with a PAC in A♭. The resulting form is a modulating period. Then arrange for some combination of instruments in your class, filling in as many inner parts as needed. Elaborate your final version with NCTs and arpeggiations.

f: i   vii°6   i6

H. Compose a double period for some solo instrument with piano accompaniment. As the diagram indicates, the first phrase stays in A, whereas the second tonicizes (or modulates to) E. Phrase 3 returns briefly to A but turns quickly to D. The fourth phrase returns to A for the final cadence.

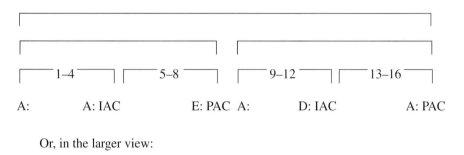

A: A: IAC   E: PAC A: D: IAC   A: PAC

Or, in the larger view:

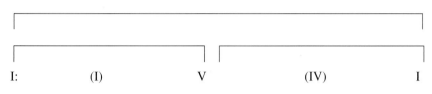

I: (I)   V   (IV)   I

The beginning of phrase 1 is given next. Compose the soprano/bass framework first.

I. Using a text of your own choosing, compose a passage for chorus (three or four parts).
    If in major, it should have a tonal scheme of I–vi–I–ii–I. If in minor, use i–VI–i–iv–i.

b. How would you explain the modulations?

Chapter 19

SOME OTHER
MODULATORY TECHNIQUES

EXERCISE 19–1

A. Analysis. (Note: Some of the modulations that follow might be of the diatonic common-chord type.)

   1. a. What three keys are implied in this excerpt?

   b. How would you explain the modulations?

   c. Continue the two-voice reduction below the score but avoid the change of register in m. 36.

   Beethoven, Piano Sonata op. 10, no. 1, I

DISK: 1 TRACK: 67

Textural reduction

2. Two modulations occur in this excerpt. Label chords and NCTs. At what point does Bach not follow the conventions of spacing discussed on pages 77–79? What is achieved by the spacing he uses? Where is a sonority used in an unusual bass position? How is the reason for this bass position related to the question about the spacing?

Bach, "Warum betrübst du dich"

DISK: 1 TRACK: 68

3. What two keys are found in this excerpt? How are they related? What is the best way to describe the modulation? Label the chords with roman numerals.

Hüllmandel, *"Un Poco Adagio"*

DISK: 1 TRACK: 69

4. Two distantly related keys are found in this passage. Label chords and NCTs.

Mozart, Don Giovanni, "Deh vieni alla finestra"

DISK: 1 TRACK: 70

5. This excerpt modulates from F major to what other key? Of excerpts 1 through 4, which modulation most closely resembles this one? In what ways? (The chords in mm. 35–36 are labeled for you because some of them involve concepts discussed in later chapters.)

Mozart, Marriage of Figaro, K. 492, "Voi che sapete"

DISK: 1 TRACK: 71

B. Analyze the harmonies implied by this soprano/bass framework. Add an alto part to
    create a three-part texture. Embellish the texture with a few NCTs, including a 4–3
    suspension. Identify the modulatory technique used.

C. Analyze the implied harmonies and then add alto and tenor parts. Enliven the texture
    with NCTs and/or arpeggiations. Identify the modulatory technique used.

D. Use the framework that follows as the basis for a repeated period. The second phrase should begin and end in D major (phrase modulation). Compose a first ending that modulates back to F using some modulatory technique discussed in this chapter. Include NCTs and arpeggiations in your final version. Score for piano or some combination of instruments found in your class.

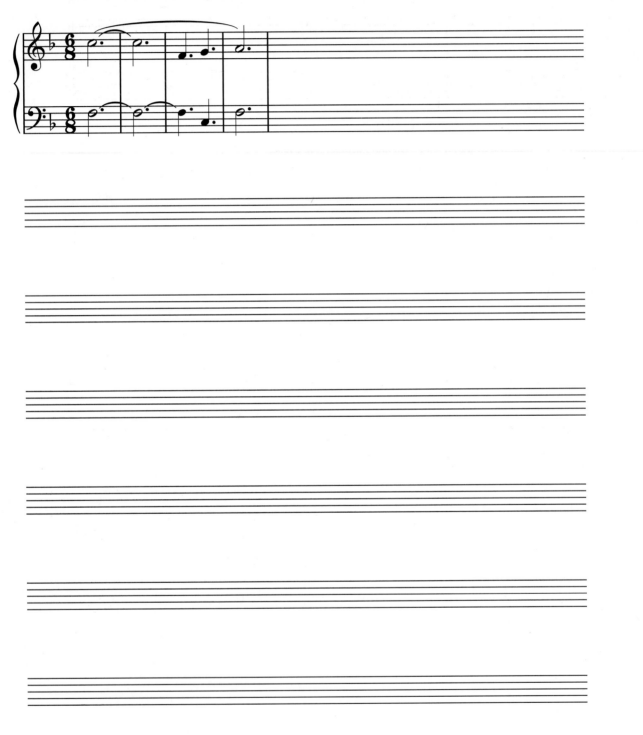

Name _____ Class _____ Date _____

E. The framework that follows is also to be used as the basis for a repeated period for piano (or other instruments). The first phrase is in E♭, and the second should be a sequential repetition of the first, in A♭. Write out the repeat of phrases 1 to 2. Use more embellishments in the repeat than you used in the first eight measures.

Chapter 20

LARGER FORMS

EXERCISE 20–1

A. Diagram this excerpt down to the phrase level and name the form. Assume all phrases
are four measures long. Answer the following questions as well:

  1. What is the form of mm. 1–8?

  2. Find and label a vii°$^4_3$/V and a vii°$^4_3$/vi.

  3. Why do you think Mozart chose to use a double stop in the violas in m. 7? (A double stop
  is a technique that allows a stringed instrument to play two notes at once.)

Mozart, *Eine kleine Nachtmusik*, III

DISK: 1 TRACK: 72

187

B. Name the form of this piece (do not diagram phrases and cadences). Watch out for written-out repeats. Also, do or answer the following:

1. Label the chords in mm. 5 to 8.

2. What chord forms the basis of mm. 33 to 39?

3. Analyze the last chord in m. 34.

4. In what measures does the "boom-chick-chick" accompaniment drop out?

  Chopin, Mazurka op. 67, no. 3

DISK: 1 TRACK: 73

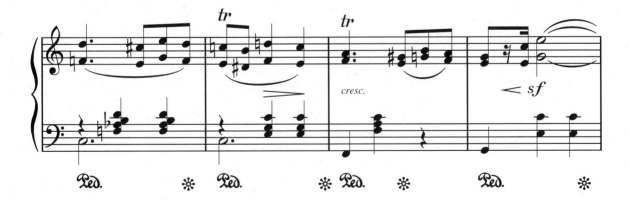

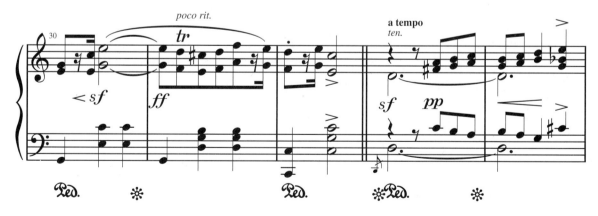

C. This excerpt is the first part of a scherzo and trio (a scherzo is much like a minuet, only faster). The trio is not shown.

   1. Diagram this scherzo at the phrase level. The key implied by mm. 17 to 20 is d minor, not A major.

   2. Identify the form. Do not be misled by the written-out repeat in mm. 9 to 16—this is a two-reprise form.

   3. Find two examples of chromatic mediant relationships.

  Beethoven, Violin Sonata op. 24, III

DISK: 1 TRACK: 74

Scherzo
La prima parte senza repetizione
Allegro molto

D. Diagram this piece down to the phrase level and name the form. Answer the following questions as well:

1. Where is a sequence involving both hands? Bracket it.

2. What does the G♯4 in m. 6 accomplish?

3. What material in mm. 10 to 22 is obviously derived from mm. 1 to 9?

March from the *Notebook for Anna Magdalena Bach*

DISK: 1 TRACK: 75

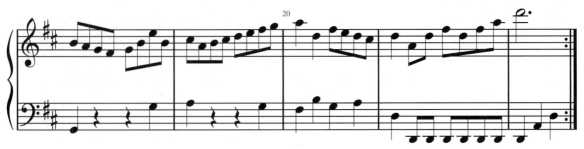

E. This excerpt, the final movement of a piano sonata, is a minuet and trio, although Haydn did not label it as such.

1. Diagram phrases and cadences, treating the minuet and trio as separate pieces. Be sure to play or listen to the music because some of the returns are disguised. (A melodically varied return of phrase *a* is still labeled phrase *a*, not phrase *a′*.)

2. Name the forms of the minuet and the trio.

3. In performance, the trio is followed by a return to the minuet (although the repeats are omitted), ending at the fermata. What is the form of the movement as a whole?

4. Find the one phrase in this movement that is not four measures long and compare it to its earlier four-measure version. How does Haydn extend this phrase?

5. Provide roman numerals for the following chords:

   a. _____ m. 17, beats 1 to 2 (in E♭)

   b. _____ m. 19, beat 3 (in E♭)

   c. _____ m. 35, beat 3 (in A♭)

   d. _____ m. 44 (in A♭)

   e. _____ m. 46, beat 3 (in A♭)

 Haydn, Piano Sonata no. 38, III

DISK: 1 TRACK: 76

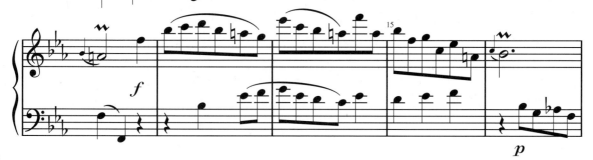

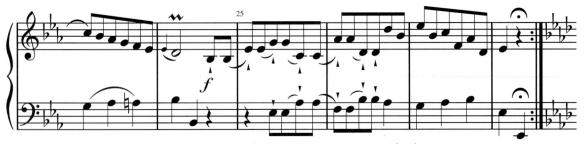

F. The following five excerpts are all taken from a piano sonata movement that can be annalyzed as a sonata form. Match the number of each example with the following parts of the sonata: *primary theme, transition, secondary theme, closing section,* and *development*. Then provide reasons for each of your answers. You should consider issues such as key, cadences, and thematic character. The home key of this movement is B♭ major.

Example 1: _____

Example 2: _____

Example 3: _____

Example 4: _____

Example 5: _____

Mozart, Piano Sonata K. 333, I

1

2

3

4

5

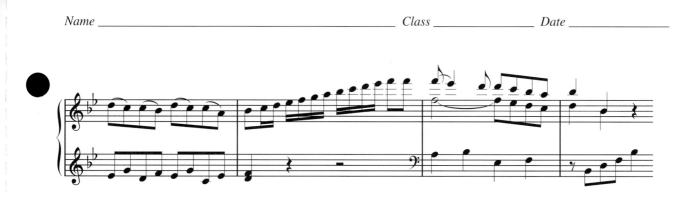

G. This excerpt, the final movement of a piano sonata, is a five-part rondo. In the score, label each of the five parts as A, B, or C, as applicable, above the staff.

What is the form of the A section?_____

Beethoven, Piano Sonata op. 49, no. 2, II

Chapter 21

MODE MIXTURE

EXERCISE 21–1

A. Notate these chords in the specified inversions. Include key signatures.

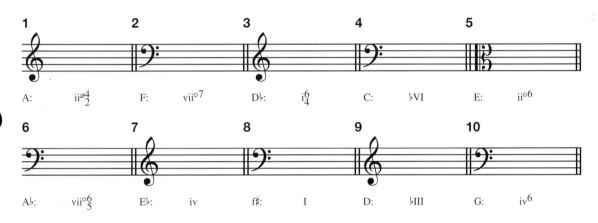

A: $\text{ii}^{\varnothing 4}_{2}$ F: $\text{vii}^{\circ 7}$ D♭: i^{6}_{4} C: ♭VI   E: $\text{ii}^{\circ 6}$

A♭: $\text{vii}^{\circ 6}_{5}$ E♭: iv   f♯: I   D: ♭III   G: iv^{6}

B. Label these chords. Include bass-position symbols.

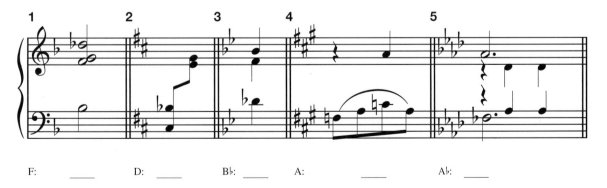

F: ____   D: ____   B♭: ____   A: ____   A♭: ____

C. Analysis.

1. Label the chords, circling the roman numerals of any borrowed chords. Label the cadence type.

DISK: 2 TRACK: 1

Brahms, Symphony no. 3, op. 90, II

2. Analyze the chords by providing roman numerals in the blanks. It may be helpful to write
in lead-sheet symbols if you run into difficulties.

Schubert, Piano Sonata in A Major, op. 120, I

DISK: 2 TRACK: 2

A: I

3. Schumann uses mode mixture in this passage to modulate from E to its minor dominant. Label all the chords and the common-chord modulation.

Schumann, "Liebeslied," op. 51, no. 5

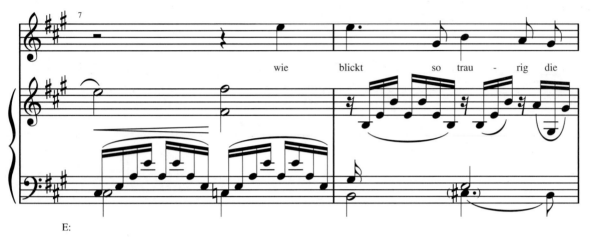

E:

4. In the following passage, Mozart uses mode mixture twice to move from E major to the very distant key of c minor; he then uses mode mixture twice more to return to E major. Label all chords, including the common-chord modulations from E to c and back. (Remember that the bass voice is always the lowest-sounding voice, so that the bass note in m. 221, for example, is the cello G, not the piano E♭.)

Mozart, Piano Trio K. 542, I

DISK: 2 TRACK: 4

5. This excerpt modulates from A♭ to some other key and then back to A♭. Label all chords and NCTs.

Schubert, Impromptu op. 90, no. 1

DISK: 2 TRACK: 5

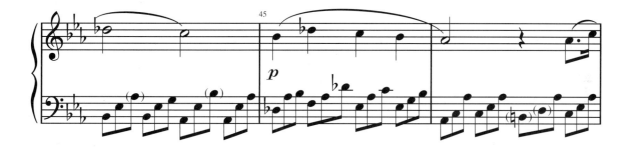

D. Part writing. Analyze the chords implied by the soprano/bass framework. Then fill in alto and tenor parts. Be sure to use the specified mode mixture.

1. Include a ii$^{\varnothing 6}_{5}$.

2. Include a iv^6 and a ii$^{\varnothing 4}_{3}$.

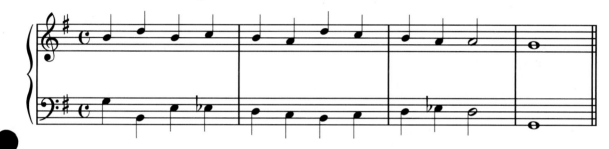

E. The first two phrases of a chorale melody are given next. A bass line is included for the first phrase. Complete the four-part texture, including in the second phrase a modulation to B♭ and a borrowed iv⁶ chord. Label all chords and circle the roman numeral of the borrowed chord. Activate the texture with NCTs and/or arpeggiations.

F. Analyze the harmonies specified by the following figured bass and then make an arrangement for SATB chorus. This passage modulates.

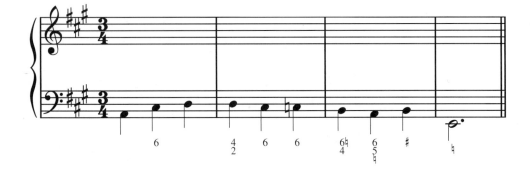

Name _____ Class _____ Date _____

G. Arrange the first modulation below for SAB chorus and the second one for SATB chorus. Activate the textures with NCTs and/or arpeggiations. Arrange the metric and rhythmic structure so that the last chord comes on a strong beat. Label chords and NCTs.

1. D: I   V   I^6 vi   iv^6 |

F: ii^6 V$^4_2$ I^6 V$^6_5$/V   I$^6_4$ V   I
              (I$^6_4$—V bracketed as V)

2. F: I   vii°$^6_5$ I^6 V$^6_5$ I   vii°$^4_3$/IV   iv^6 |

b♭: i^6 iv   i$^6_4$ V   i
              (i$^6_4$—V bracketed as V)

H. Use the framework that follows as the basis for the beginning of a passage that starts in F major and modulates to D♭ major by means of mode mixture. Score for piano or for some combination of instruments in your class.

Chapter 22

THE NEAPOLITAN CHORD

EXERCISE 22–1

A. Label the chords with lead-sheet symbols and roman numerals.

Ab: _____   e: _____   Bb: _____   f: _____   F#: _____

Eb: _____   D: _____   g: _____   A: _____   b: _____

B. Provide key signatures. Then notate the chords and label them with lead-sheet symbols.

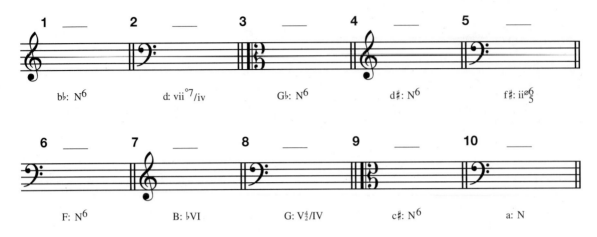

1 _____ 2 _____ 3 _____ 4 _____ 5 _____

bb: N⁶   d: vii°⁷/iv   G♭: N⁶   d♯: N⁶   f♯: ii⌀$^6_5$

6 _____ 7 _____ 8 _____ 9 _____ 10 _____

F: N⁶   B: ♭VI   G: V$^4_2$/IV   c♯: N⁶   a: N

Name ______________________ Class ____________ Date ____________

C. Analysis.

1. Label chords and NCTs.

Chopin, Prelude op. 28, no. 20

DISK: 2 TRACK: 6

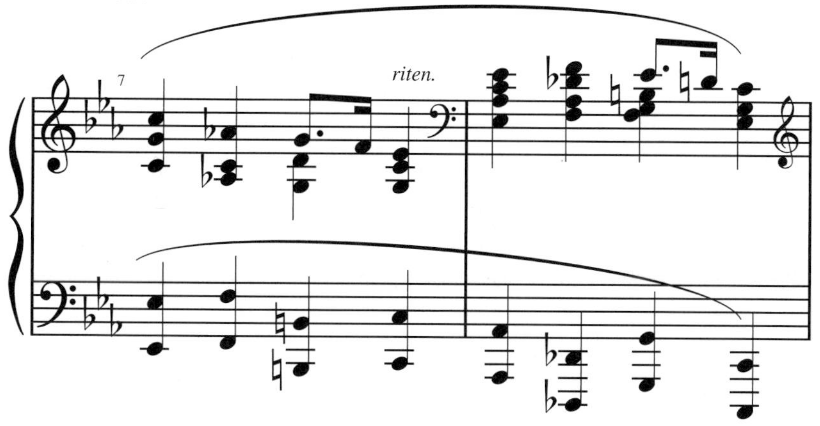

2. Label the chords in this modulating excerpt.

Beethoven, Piano Sonata op. 27, no. 2, I

DISK: 2 TRACK: 7

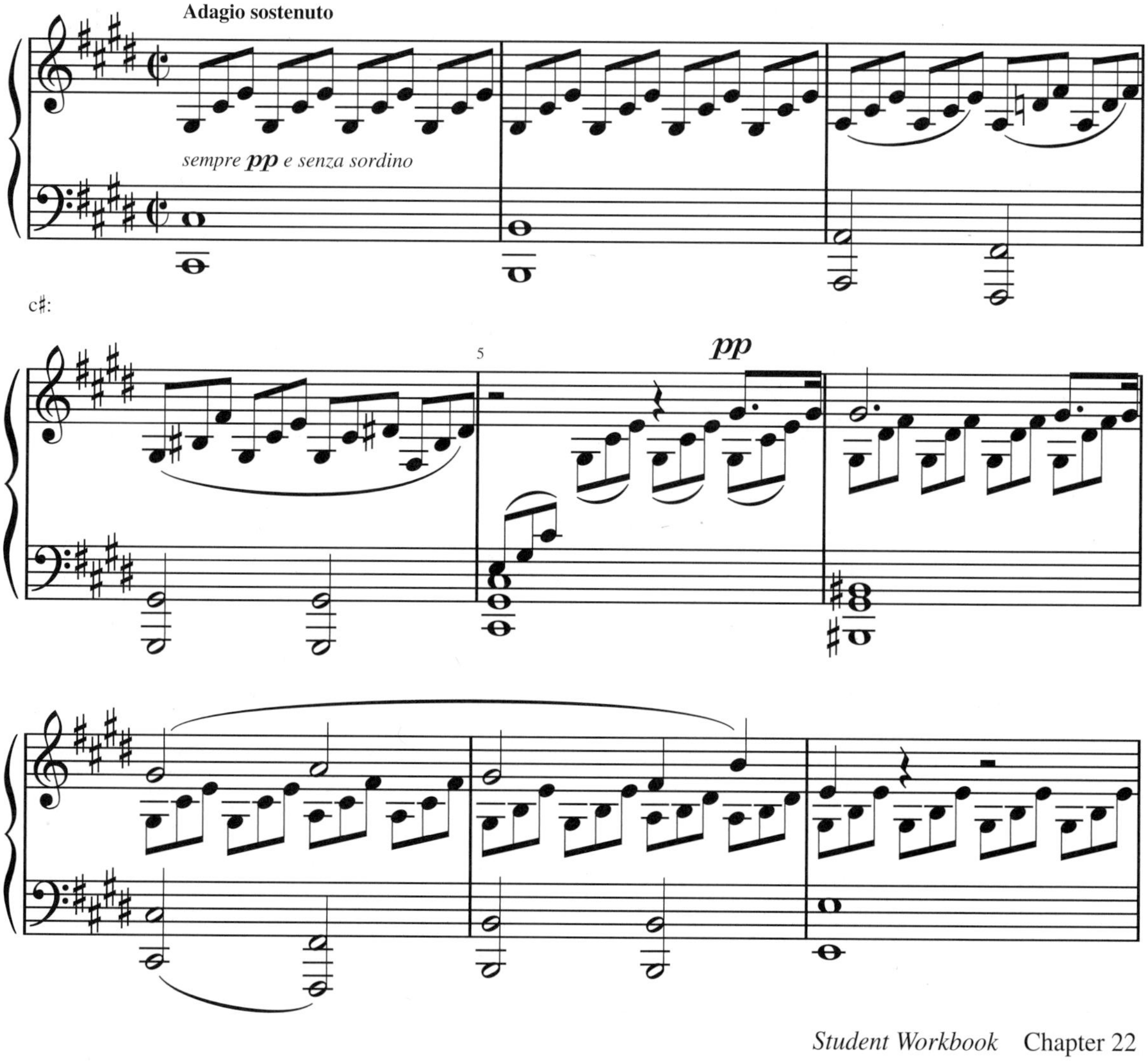

3. Label the chords in this excerpt.

Schubert, String Quartet op. 168, I

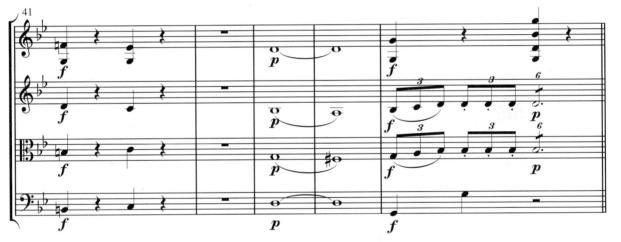

4. This beautiful and moving theme illustrates the expressive power of the Neapolitan chord. Label all the chords and NCTs. The B♯ in m. 6 is not a chord tone but instead delays the arrival of C♯. By the time the C♯ arrives, however, the harmony has moved on. Does something similar happen in m. 8, or is the A♯ a chord tone? Be sure to listen to or play this example.

 Mozart, Piano Concerto K. 488, II

DISK: 2 TRACK: 9

5. At this point in Schubert's famous "Erlkönig," the evil personality of the title character is finally expressed, with the help of the Neapolitan triad. Label the chords.

Schubert, "Erlkönig," op. 1

DISK: 2 TRACK: 10

d:

lie - be dich, mich reizt dei - ne schö - ne Ge - stalt; und

bist du nicht wil - lig, so brauch ich Ge - walt."

Name ______________________ Class ____________ Date ____________

6. At the end of the song, the father's frantic ride comes to an end, and we hear the Neapolitan again. Label the chords.

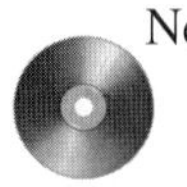

Schubert, "Erlkönig," op. 1

DISK: 2 TRACK: 11

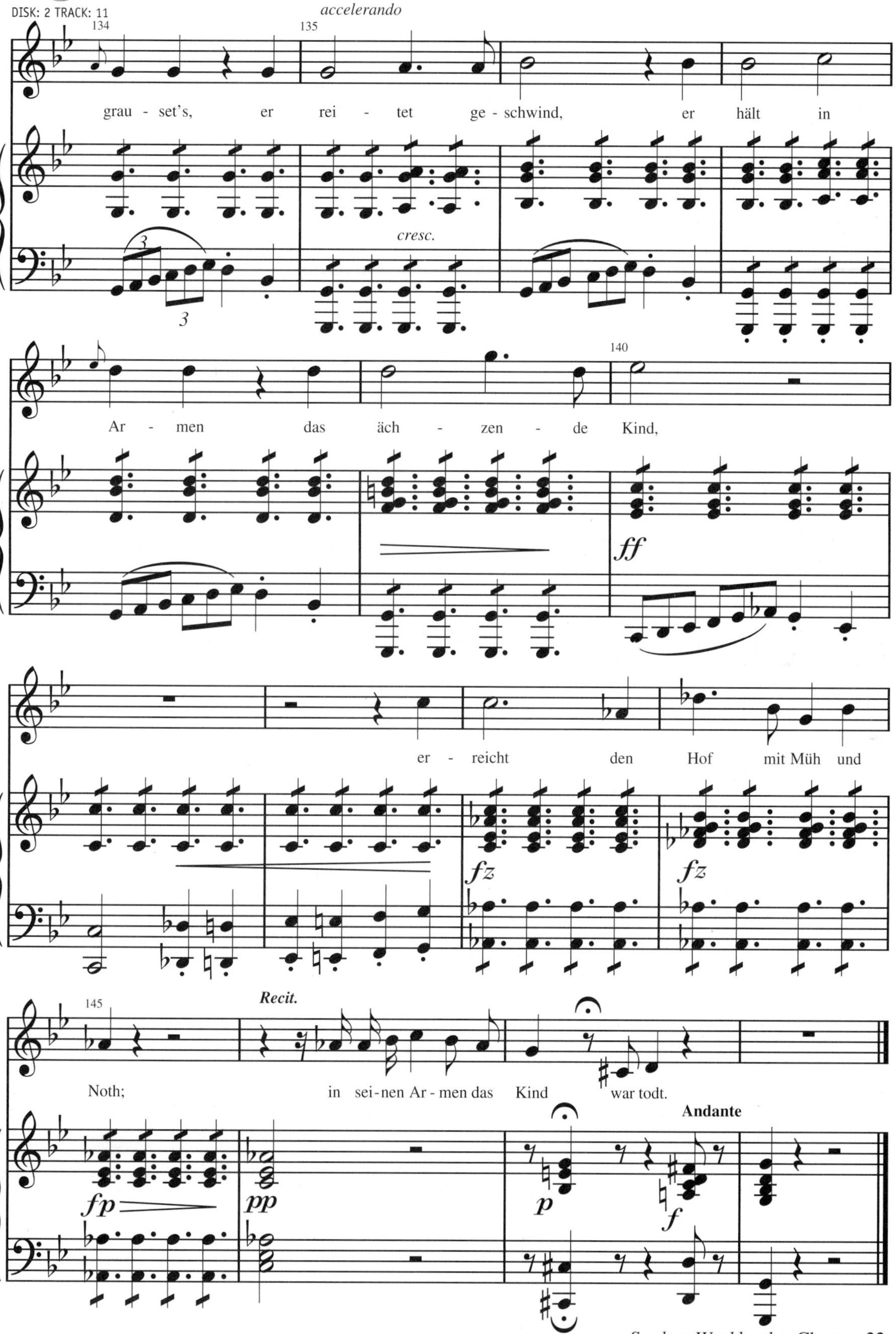

7. Mode mixture is involved in this excerpt in modulations to the key of the Neapolitan and back again. Label all chords, including common chords for both modulations.

Beethoven, Rondo op. 51, no. 1

DISK: 2 TRACK: 12

C: I

D. For each exercise, provide the correct key signature and notate the specified chords preceding and following the N⁶. Use the given three- or four-part texture in each case.

b: iv N^6 V   e: VI N^6 V^4_2 c: iv N^6 i^6_4 V   f#: i^6 N^6 V^4_2

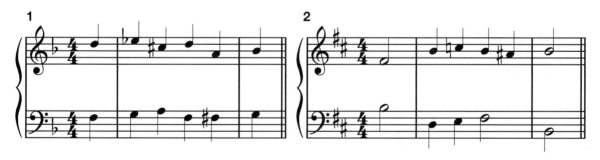

d: i N^6 V   c#:   VI N^6 vii^{o7}/V g: iv N^6 vii^{o7}/V f: V^7/N N V^7

E. Analyze the harmonies implied by the soprano/bass framework. Then fill in inner voices to make a four-part texture. Each exercise should contain a Neapolitan chord.

d:

b:

3

c:

F. Analyze the chords specified by this figured bass and then make an arrangement for SATB chorus.

G. Make settings of the following progressions for three or four parts, as specified. Arrange the rhythmic/metric scheme so that the final chord of each progression comes on a strong beat. Activate the texture with arpeggiations and/or NCTs.

1. (4 parts) g: i V i^6 i VI V$^4_2$/N N^6 vii$^{\circ 7}$/V $\underbrace{i^6_4 \qquad V}_{V}$ i

2. (3 parts) e: i V$^4_2$/iv iv^6 i$^6_4$ N^6 V$^4_2$ i^6 vii$^{\circ 6}$ i

3. (4 parts) Eb: I I^6 vi ii V $\overline{\quad I^6 \quad}$

                                        d: N^6 vii$^{\circ 7}$/V $\underbrace{i^6_4 \qquad V^7}_{V}$ i

4. (3 parts) b: i V VI i^6 N^6

                                  G: IV^6 V$^6_5$ I V I

H. Use the framework that follows as the first phrase of a three-phrase excerpt having the following structure:

b: HC   f#:   HC   PAC

Phrase 2 modulates to f# minor. Phrase 3 remains in f# minor and contains a Neapolitan triad. After completing the framework, make a more elaborate version for piano or for some combination of instruments in your class.

I.   Make a setting of the following text or another text of your choice for three-part chorus.
     Include in your setting examples of the following:

     Neapolitan triad

     Mode mixture

     Common-chord modulation

Your composition should begin and end in the same key. Be sure to include a harmonic
analysis.

     A storm of white petals,
     Buds throwing open baby fists
     Into hands of broad flowers.

     —From "The Year," in *Cornhuskers* by Carl Sandburg, copyright 1918 by Holt,
     Rinehart and Winston, Inc.; renewed 1946 by Carl Sandburg. Reprinted by permis-
     sion of Harcourt Brace & Company.

Chapter 23

AUGMENTED SIXTH CHORDS 1

EXERCISE 23–1

A. For each exercise that follows, provide the key signature, and then notate $\sharp\hat{4}$ to $\hat{5}$ on the top staff and $\hat{6}$ to $\hat{5}$ (or, in major, $\flat\hat{6}$ to $\hat{5}$) on the bottom staff. Finally, show an analysis of the implied chords as in the example.

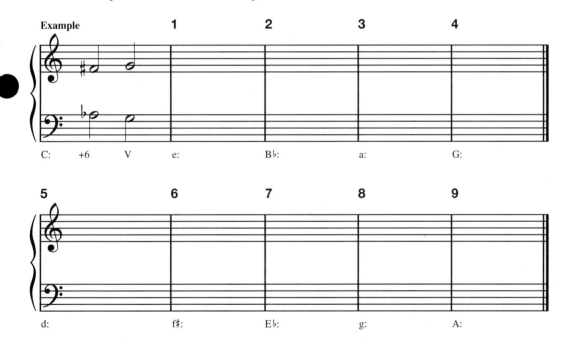

Example	1	2	3	4

C: +6   V   e: Bb: a: G:

5	6	7	8	9

d: f#:   Eb: g: A:

B. Label each chord, using bass-position symbols where appropriate.

c♯: _____   b: _____   f: _____   E♭: _____   D: _____

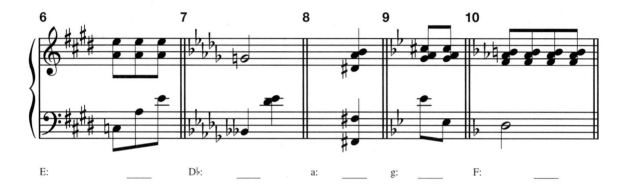

E: _____   D♭: _____   a: _____   g: _____   F: _____

C. Notate each chord in close position. Augmented sixth chords should be in their cus-
    tomary bass position ($\hat{6}$ in the bass in minor, ♭$\hat{6}$ in major). Include key signatures.

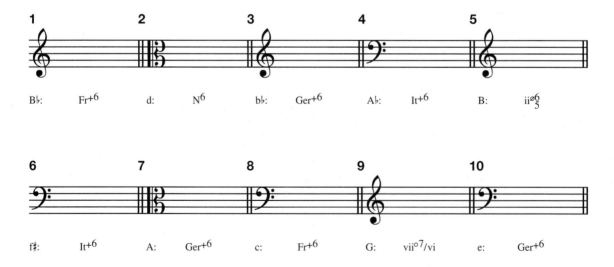

B♭:   Fr+6   d: N6   b♭:   Ger+6   A♭:   It+6   B: ii∅$^6_5$

f♯:   It+6   A: Ger+6   c: Fr+6   G: vii°7/vi   e: Ger+6

D. Label the chords in each example that follows. Also, discuss the details of the resolution of each augmented sixth chord. Do $\sharp\hat{4}$ and $\flat\hat{6}$ follow their expected resolutions to
$\hat{5}$? How are parallel 5ths avoided in the Ger^{+6} resolution(s)?

1. Measures 2 to 5 of this excerpt are in d minor, although the key of VI (B$\flat$) is strongly
tonicized in mm. 2 to 3 (the second chord in m. 2 should be analyzed as a secondary
function of VI). Common-chord modulations to two other keys occur in mm. 5 to 11.

Schumann, "Sehnsucht," op. 51, no. 1

DISK: 2 TRACK: 13

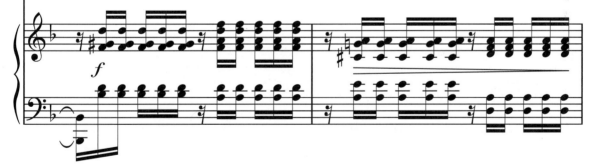

2. This excerpt begins and ends in g minor, but it contains modulations to two other keys (or tonicizations of two other chords). How do those keys relate to the "parent" tonality of g minor?

Schumann, "Die beiden Grenadiere," op. 49, no. 1

DISK: 2 TRACK: 14

wohl ob der kläg-li-chen Kun-de. Der Ei-ne sprach: "Wie weh wird

mir, wie brennt mei-ne al - te Wun-de!" Der An-dre sprach: "Das Lied ist

aus, auch ich möcht' mit dir ster-ben, doch hab' ich Weib und

Kind zu Haus, die oh - ne mich ver - der - ben." "Was schert mich Weib,

3. This very chromatic excerpt from an early Mozart string quartet contains an augmented sixth chord that resolves quite irregularly. Before you begin to label the chords, review the use of the subdominant chord in minor on pp. 64–65 and 243.

Mozart, String Quartet K. 168, II (piano arrangement)

DISK: 2 TRACK: 15

C:

4. This excerpt begins in C major and modulates. Where is there a 9–8 suspension?

Haydn, String Quartet op. 74, no. 3, II

DISK: 2 TRACK: 16

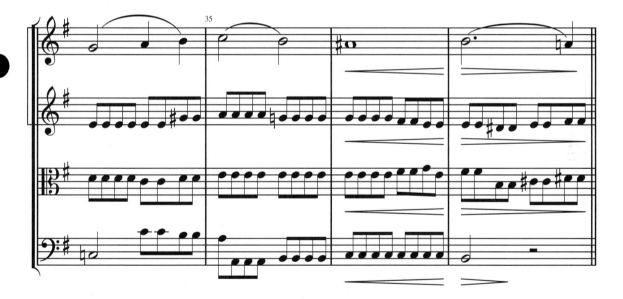

5. This excerpt modulates to the dominant, passing through another key on the way. The first chord in m. 8 is spelled enharmonically (imagine a G♮ instead of the F𝄪). Be sure to analyze a chord on beat 2 of m. 8.

Schumann, Tragödie, op. 136, no. 3

6. The slow tempo of this theme allows some measures to contain several chords. In the first measure, for example, each bass note is harmonized by a new chord, with the exception of the B2. Discuss the various uses of the pitch class G♯/A♭ in this excerpt.

 Beethoven, String Trio op. 9, no. 3, II

DISK: 2 TRACK: 18

Name _____ Class _____ Date _____

E.   Supply the missing voices for each of the following fragments. All are four-part textures.

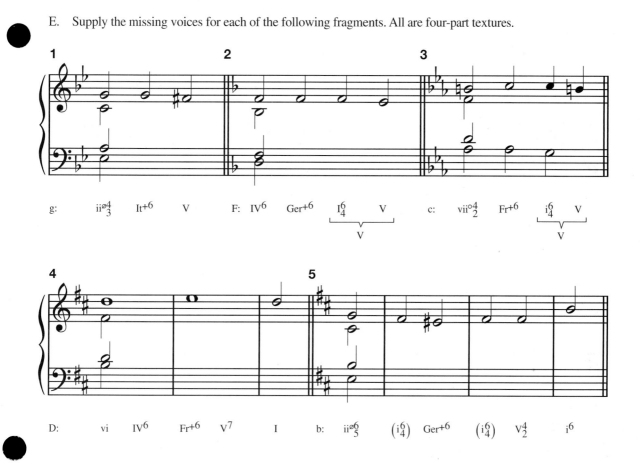

D: vi   IV⁶   Fr⁺⁶   V⁷   I   b: ii°⁶₅   (i⁶₄)   Ger⁺⁶   (i⁶₄)   V⁴₂   i⁶

F.   Complete these harmonizations, adding one or two inner voices, as specified.

e: i   Ger⁺⁶   i   E♭:   I   It⁺⁶   I

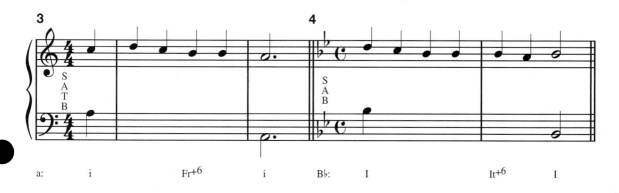

a: i   Fr⁺⁶   i   B♭:   I   It⁺⁶   I

G. Analyze the harmonies specified by this figured bass and then make an arrangement for SATB chorus.

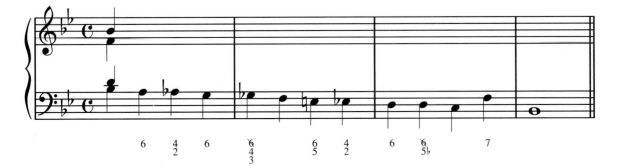

H. Analyze the harmonies implied by this soprano/bass framework, being sure to include an It^{+6}. Then fill in the inner voices, following good voice-leading procedures. There are no NCTs in the bass and soprano lines.

I. Given next are mm. 1 to 2 of a four-measure phrase. Continue the passage to make a period (parallel or contrasting) that ends with a PAC in the key of the dominant. Include an augmented sixth chord.

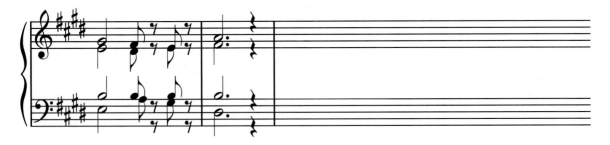

Chapter 24

AUGMENTED SIXTH CHORDS 2

EXERCISE 24–1

A.   Label the chords in the keys indicated.

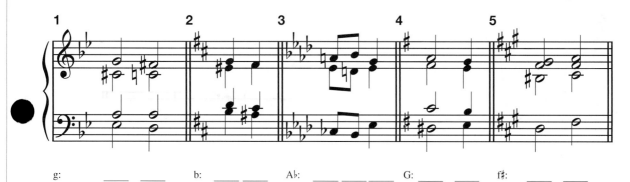

g: ____ ____   b: ____ ____   A♭: ____ ____   G: ____ ____   f♯: ____ ____

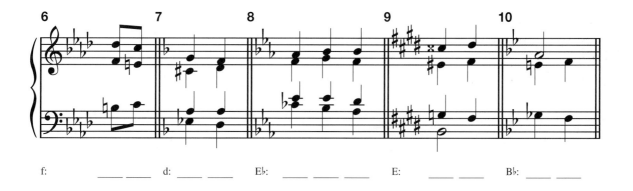

f: ____ ____   d: ____ ____   E♭: ____ ____   E: ____ ____   B♭: ____ ____

B. Analysis.

1. Label the chords in this example. Measures 10 to 12 could be analyzed in terms of secondary functions or as a modulation.

Tchaikovsky, "The Nurse's Tale," op. 39, no. 19

DISK: 2 TRACK: 19

2. In a number of his works, Scriabin used the chord found at the end of the first measure. Label the chords.

Scriabin, *Tragic Poem*, op. 34

DISK: 2 TRACK: 20

3. This excerpt will give you practice with both alto and tenor clefs. Label all chords and
NCTs.

 Schubert, String Trio D. 471

DISK: 2 TRACK: 21

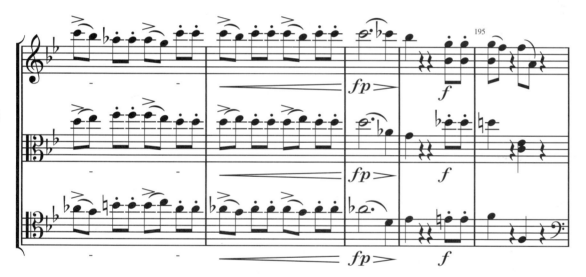

4. As you might guess, an enharmonically spelled $^+$6 chord occurs in this excerpt. Label the chords.

Koffman, "Swinging Shepherd Blues"

DISK: 2 TRACK: 22

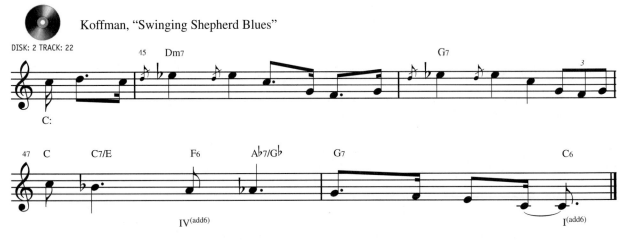

5. This example begins in A and modulates. Label the chords.

Schumann, "Novellette," op. 21, no. 7 (simplified texture)

DISK: 2 TRACK: 23

6. Label the chords.

Beethoven, Violin Sonata op. 23, III

DISK: 2 TRACK: 24

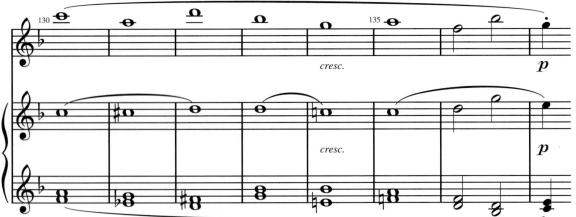

Chapter 25

ENHARMONIC SPELLINGS AND ENHARMONIC MODULATIONS

EXERCISE 25–1

A. Analyze the given chord. Then show any possible enharmonic reinterpretation(s) of that chord, keeping the same key signature. The enharmonic reinterpretation should involve a new key, not just an enharmonically equivalent key (such as g♯ and a♭). Number 1 is supplied as an example.

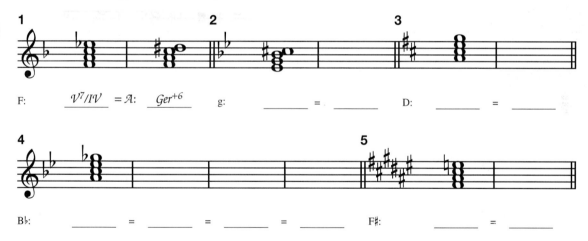

F: $\underline{V^7/IV}$ = A: $\underline{Ger^{+6}}$ g: _____ = _____   D: _____ = _____

Bb: _____ = _____ = _____ = _____   F♯: _____ = _____

B. Each of the following short passages contains an enharmonic modulation. Analyze each passage after playing it slowly at the piano and listening for the point of modulation. Do not try to analyze these passages without hearing them.

2

3

C. Analyze the progressions implied by these soprano and bass lines and fill in the inner voices. Analyze enharmonic common chords where indicated.

Use two different chords on the last beat of m. 2 and the first beat of m. 3 in Exercise 1.

1

b: i   :   V

2

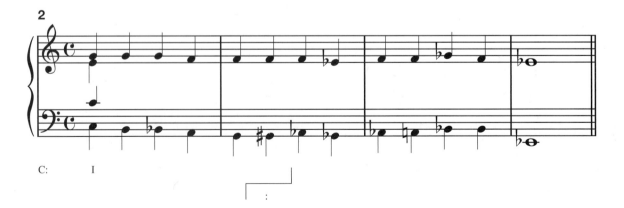

C: I   :

D. Compose short passages similar to those in Part B. The given chord is to serve as the common chord in an enharmonic modulation. (Hint: As you sketch out your progression, notate the given chord first. Then find satisfactory ways to lead into and away from that chord.)

1. G to B. Common chord: V^7/IV in G.

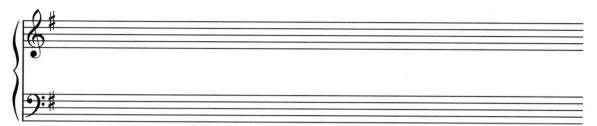

2. b to B♭. Common chord: $vii^{\circ 7}$/iv in b.

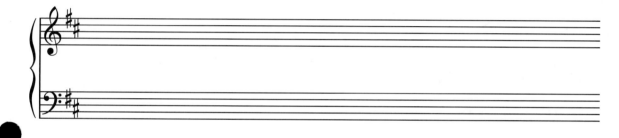

3. B♭ to E. Common chord: $vii^{\circ \frac{6}{5}}$ in B♭.

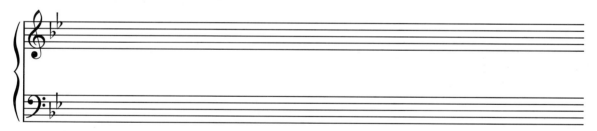

4. E to F. Common chord: Ger^{+6} in E.

E. Analysis. Be sure to play as much as you can of each excerpt.

1. This passage modulates from f♯ minor to A♭ major by way of E major. The bass notes are found above the *"Ped,"* markings—the other notes in the bass clef are arpeggiations into inner voices. Label all the chords, including common chords for both modulations.

Chopin, Nocturne op. 27, no. 1

DISK: 2 TRACK: 25

2. This excerpt begins in g minor. Label all the chords.

Beethoven, Piano Sonata op. 13, I

DISK: 2 TRACK: 26

3. This excerpt is from the end of the exposition and the beginning of the development of a movement in sonata form (review pp. 344–354). The final cadence of the last B theme is shown in the first few measures of the excerpt (in E♭ major). The music then leads to a modulation to C minor in the first ending and to A minor in the second ending. Notice that the sonority first heard in m. 76 is used again twice, each time in a different way. (Bonus question: what *other* sonority in these measures is treated enharmonically?)

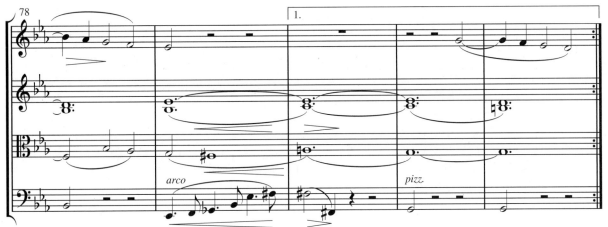

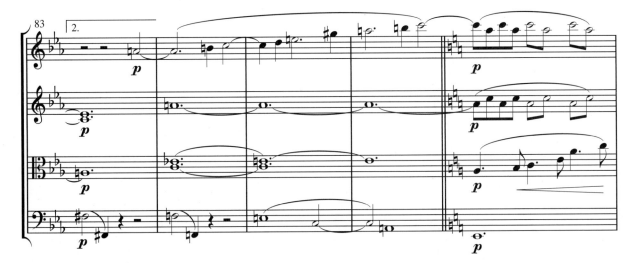

4. The next excerpt is quite challenging. Label both chords and NCTs. You might find it helpful to label the chords with lead-sheet symbols before assigning roman numerals.

   Haydn, String Quartet op. 76, no. 6, II

DISK: 2 TRACK: 28

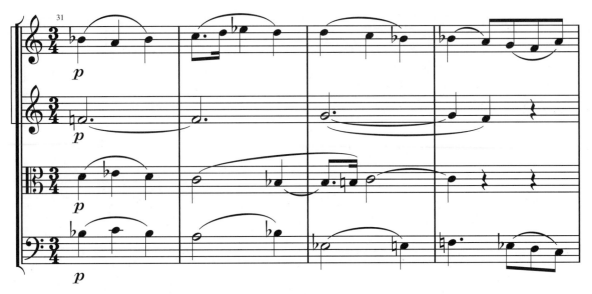

5. This dance modulates from D♭ to A and back again. Although both modulations involve enharmonicism, only one of them is a true enharmonic modulation—the other uses enharmonic spellings for convenience.

a. Label all the chords, including two common-chord modulations.

b. Label the enharmonic modulation.

c. Name the form of this piece.

Schubert, Originaltänze, op. 9 (D. 365), no. 14

DISK: 2 TRACK: 29

F. Use mm. 31 to 34 of Part E, number 4, as the first phrase of an eight-measure parallel
    period. The second phrase should include an enharmonic modulation to a foreign key.

G. Compose the beginning of a song with piano accompaniment, using a text of your choice. Include two enharmonic modulations, one of them using a Ger^{+6} chord, the other a diminished seventh chord.

Chapter 26

FURTHER ELEMENTS OF THE HARMONIC VOCABULARY

EXERCISE 26–1

A. In each fragment that follows, analyze the given chord. Then notate the specified chord in such a way that it leads smoothly into the given chord with acceptable voice leading. Some of the problems use a five-part texture for simpler voice leading.

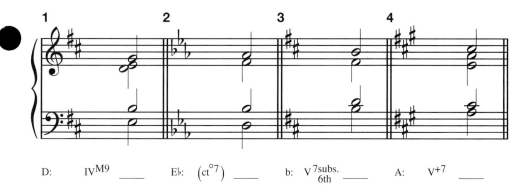

D: IV^{M9} _____   E♭:   (ct$^{°7}$) _____   b: V^{7}subs. _____   A: V^{+7} _____
                                                         6th

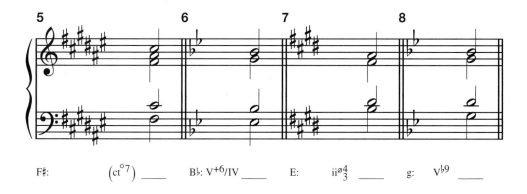

F♯:   (ct$^{°7}$) _____   B♭: V^{+6}/IV _____   E: ii$^{ø4}_{3}$ _____   g: V$^{♭9}$ _____

B. Compose four short passages for piano, each one making use of a different progression from Part A. The half-note durations do not need to be retained, but use the same voice leading.

C. Analysis. Throughout this section highlight (using arrows or whatever is convenient)
   any occurrences of the chords discussed in this chapter.

   1. Label chords and NCTs.

   Schumann, *Humoresque,* op. 20

   DISK: 2 TRACK: 30

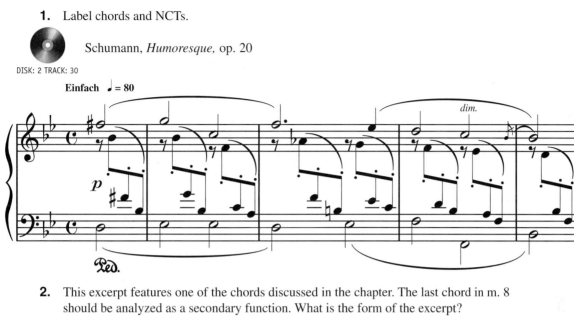

   2. This excerpt features one of the chords discussed in the chapter. The last chord in m. 8
   should be analyzed as a secondary function. What is the form of the excerpt?

   Chopin, Nocturne, op. 32, no. 2

   DISK: 2 TRACK: 31

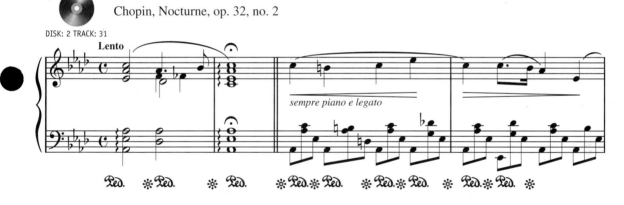

3. a. Analyze this excerpt in f minor throughout. One of the chords is best analyzed as a chord with an added 6th.

b. Put parentheses around NCTs and be prepared to discuss them.

c. Diagram the phrase structure and label the form. Assume four-measure phrases.

Chopin, Mazurka op. 63, no. 2

DISK: 2 TRACK: 32

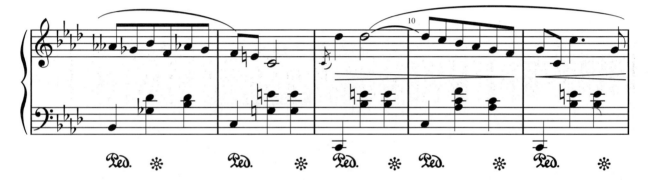

4. The following excerpt is written for barbershop quartet. The treble clef part sounds an octave lower, and the melody is given to the second tenor (the bottom voice in the treble clef). Music for barbershop quartet frequently uses ct°7 chords, and you will find some in this excerpt, including one that embellishes a secondary dominant. Label all chords and NCTs, analyzing in A♭ throughout.

Ayer (arr. by Campbell), "Oh! You Beautiful Doll"

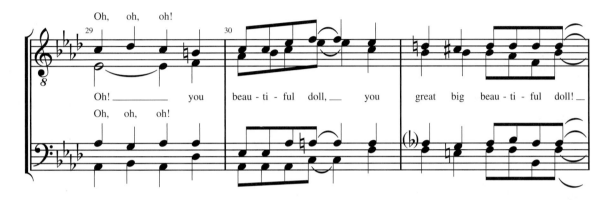

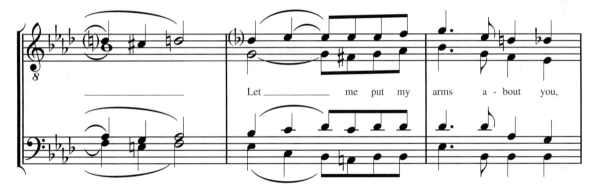

© Rob Campbell, 1987.

5. Harmonic sequences occupy most of this excerpt. Find the two sequences and bracket each occurrence of the sequential patterns. If it is possible to do so, label the chords in the sequences with roman numerals, perhaps in terms of shifting tonalities. Discuss briefly the large-scale harmonic/melodic function of each sequence. In other words, just what does each sequence accomplish harmonically and melodically? (An excerpt from the beginning of this song appears on p. 153.)

Schumann, "Die Löwenbraut," op. 31, no. 1

DISK: 2 TRACK: 33

6. This familiar excerpt is easier to listen to than to analyze. The transpositions do not make the analysis any easier—clarinets in A and horns in F—nor do the four clefs in use. Do your best with the score (after all, conductors face this sort of problem every day), then check your work with the piano reduction that follows the excerpt.

Tchaikovsky, Symphony no. 6, op. 74, I

DISK: 2 TRACK: 34

Piano reduction

7. The chord in m. 4 should be analyzed in two ways: the way in which we expect it to resolve when we first hear it and the way it actually functions.

Schubert, *Schwanengesang,* "Kriegers Ahnung"

DISK: 2 TRACK: 35

8. This excerpt ends with an enharmonic modulation leading to a cadence that implies the key of e, although it is not confirmed by the following phrase.

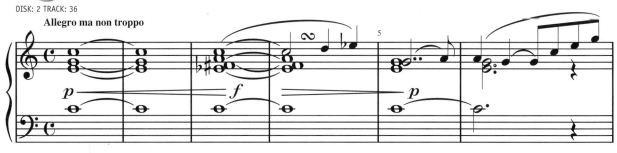

Schubert, String Quintet, op. 163, I (piano reduction)

DISK: 2 TRACK: 36

9. Label with roman numerals the two chords in this excerpt that are the most important structurally. The other chords are simultaneities connecting the structural chords. Label them with lead-sheet symbols. If any of these chords imply fleeting tonicizations, indicate this with roman numerals. The chord in m. 2 could be heard as a g triad with raised *and* lowered 5th (G–B♭–D♭–D♯) because the E♭ ascends chromatically to E, as we would expect D♯ to do. Find another chord in this passage that could be interpreted similarly.

 Wagner, *Siegfried,* act I (piano-vocal score)

DISK: 2 TRACK: 37

10. In some ways this excerpt pushes traditional harmony toward its limits, especially through its disregard for conventional resolutions of dissonance. Nevertheless, the entire passage can be analyzed reasonably well in traditional terms. Label all the chords. Which portion of the excerpt is the most unconventional in terms of dissonance treatment?

    Grieg, "The Mountain Maid," op. 67, no. 2

DISK: 2 TRACK: 38

Chapter 27

TONAL HARMONY IN THE LATE NINETEENTH CENTURY

EXERCISE 27–1

A. Examine the first 25 measures of the opening of *Tannhäuser,* given next, and do the following:

1. The opening eight measures show rather traditional harmonic function. Analyze these measures, using roman numerals (do all work on the music).

2. The following eight measures, which may also be analyzed with roman numerals, show less traditional harmonic movement. Cite at least three instances in which this is true (show measure number).

    a. _____

    b. _____

    c. _____

3. Analyze the sequence that begins at m. 17 and continues through m. 21.

m. 17	m. 18	m. 19	m. 20	m. 21	

   Use lead-sheet symbols, roman numerals, or a mixture of both, whichever seems appropriate. Circle those chords that are most strongly tonicized. How is such tonicization accomplished?

   Wagner, *Tannhäuser,* Prelude to act I (piano reduction)

DISK: 2 TRACK: 39

267

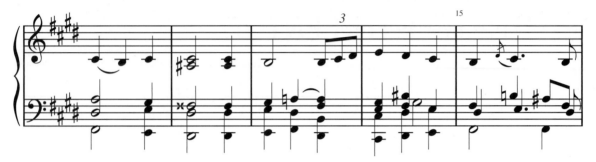

B. Analyze the following chromatic sequences, then continue each as indicated.

1

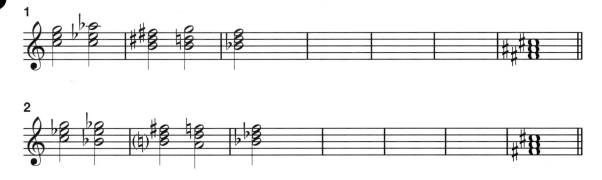

2

Select one of the preceding sequence patterns to serve as the basis for a piano composition. You might want to create a melody over the background of block chords or perhaps modify the texture of the harmonies themselves. Nonessential or embellishing
chords may be inserted within the sequence for the purpose of color.

C. Continue the following sequences as indicated. Then select one to serve as the harmonic basis for a piano or vocal composition in the style of one of the post-Romantic
composers studied. Strive for contrapuntal interest and smooth voice leading.

1

2

3

D. Examine the following excerpt.

   1. The opening key is designated as E major. What is interesting about the structure of the scale that forms the basis for mm. 2 and 3? _____

      _____   _____

      _____

   2. Provide roman numeral analysis for m. 2. _____
      In what way does the music in mm. 10 to 11 suggest more traditional treatment of tonality?

      _____

      _____

   3. Describe the modulatory procedure that takes place in mm. 12 to 13. _____

      _____

      _____

   4. Name the key introduced in m. 14. _____

      What is its relationship to the opening key? _____

   5. Name two other keys hinted at between mm. 1 and 14. _____

      and _____ These keys represent what relationship to each other and to

      the opening key? _____

Wolf, "Die ihr schwebet um diese Palmen"

DISK: 2 TRACK: 40

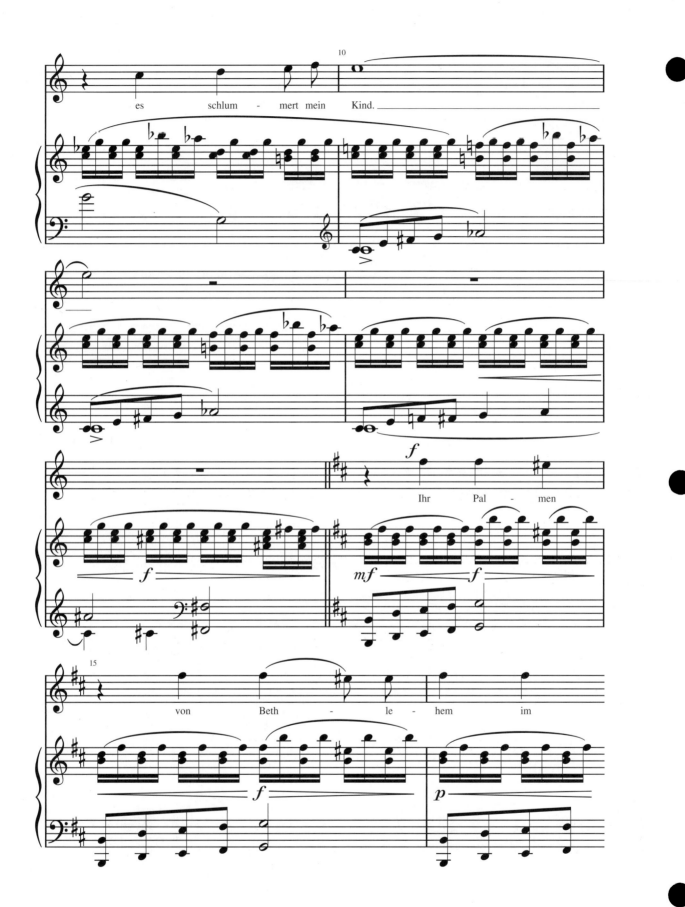

E.

1. Is there a clear tonal center in the opening five bars of the following excerpt? If so, what is it and how is it defined?_____

   _____

   _____

2. Using lead-sheet symbols, name the two sonorities found in mm. 6 and 7. _____

   and _____ In what way could these chords be said to suggest functional harmony in the key of D major, which ultimately concludes the excerpt, as well as

   the piece? _____

   _____

3. What roman numerals are used in mm. 9 to 12 to prepare the cadence in D major?

   | m. 9 | m. 10 | m. 11 | m. 12 |

Wolf, "Verschwiegene Liebe"

DISK: 2 TRACK: 41

Sanfte Bewegung und immer sehr zart

ausdrucksvoll und weich

leise

Ü - ber Wip - fel und Saa - ten

in den Glanz ___ hin-ein, ___ wer mag sie er - ra - ten, wer

hol - te sie ein? ___ Ge -

dan - ken sich wie - gen, die Nacht ist ver-schwie - gen, Ge -

Name _____ Class _____ Date _____

dan - ken sind frei. Er -

F. The first 10 measures of *Reverie* may be analyzed with traditional roman numerals (if
    you watch out for enharmonic respellings). Do so, then comment on reasons for the
    rather contemporary sound of the piece.

    Payne, *Reverie*

DISK: 2 TRACK: 42

_____

_____

_____

_____

_____

G.

1. The following excerpt begins and ends in E major. What is unusual about the manner in which the key is established in mm. 10 to 13? _____

_____

_____

2. Label on the music the harmonies found in mm. 14 to 22. Use lead-sheet symbols for your analysis.

3. What five-chord succession within mm. 14 to 22 represents an "omnibus" fragment?

_____

4. In what way is the approach to the closing E major harmony unusual? _____

_____

_____

5. By what means does Fauré make it convincing, nonetheless?

_____

_____

_____

Fauré, "Chanson d'Amour," op. 27, no. 1 (mm. 10–22)

DISK: 2 TRACK: 43

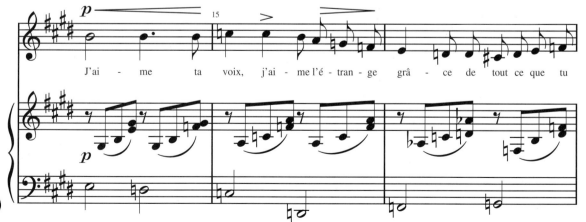

dis,　　　　　O ma re-belle,　　　ô - mon cher an　-　ge,

Mon en - fer　et mon pa - ra - dis!　　　J'ai - me tes yeux

H.

1. In the *Siegfried* excerpt, analyze one essential harmony for each of the first 11 measures of the excerpt.

m. 1	m. 2	m. 3	m. 4	m. 5	m. 6	m. 7	m. 8	m. 9	m. 10	m. 11

2. Name at least three keys (including the first one) that are established throughout the course of this excerpt. Show the measure numbers.

_____   _____   _____

3. Show two instances in which modulation is effected by deceptive resolution, either of chords or of single pitches. Describe the process that takes place.

_____

_____

_____

Wagner, *Siegfried* (act III, scene 3)

DISK: 2 TRACK: 44

I.

1. What is unusual about the treatment of tonality in the opening four measures of the Franck prelude? _____

_____

_____

2. Describe the nontraditional treatment of the dominant seventh sonority in mm. 5 to 9 of the excerpt. _____

_____

_____

3. In what way is the musical style significantly influenced by the treatment of nonharmonic material? Consider both single tones and vertical sonorities. _____

_____

_____

_____

Franck, *Prelude, Aria, and Finale for Piano* (Prelude)

DISK: 2 TRACK: 45

J. The following excerpt is taken from the *Barcarolle,* op. 17, no. 6, by Richard Strauss (mm. 21–30).

1. What key is implied by the melody in the opening four bars? _____

2. What means does Strauss employ to negate that tonal implication and, indeed, any clear

    tonal implication? _____

    _____

    _____

    _____

3. Show the underlying harmonic structure of mm. 25 to 29, using lead-sheet symbols.

m. 25	m. 26	m. 27	m. 28	m. 29

4. Within the preceding passage, locate and describe at least three examples of deceptive resolution that serve to make the chord succession convincing.

    a. _____

    b. _____

    c. _____

Strauss, *Barcarolle,* op. 17, no. 6

DISK: 2 TRACK: 46

MATERIALS AND TECHNIQUES

EXERCISE 28–1

A. Add the appropriate accidentals to create the modal scale indicated.

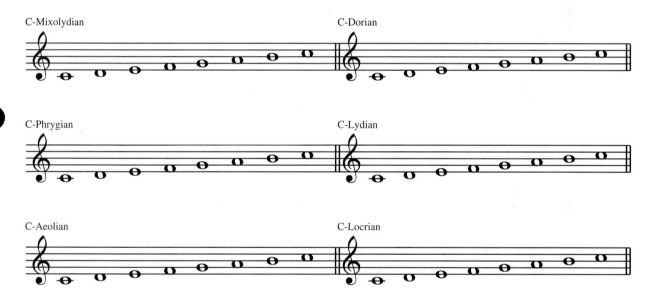

B. Add the appropriate accidentals to create the modal scale indicated.

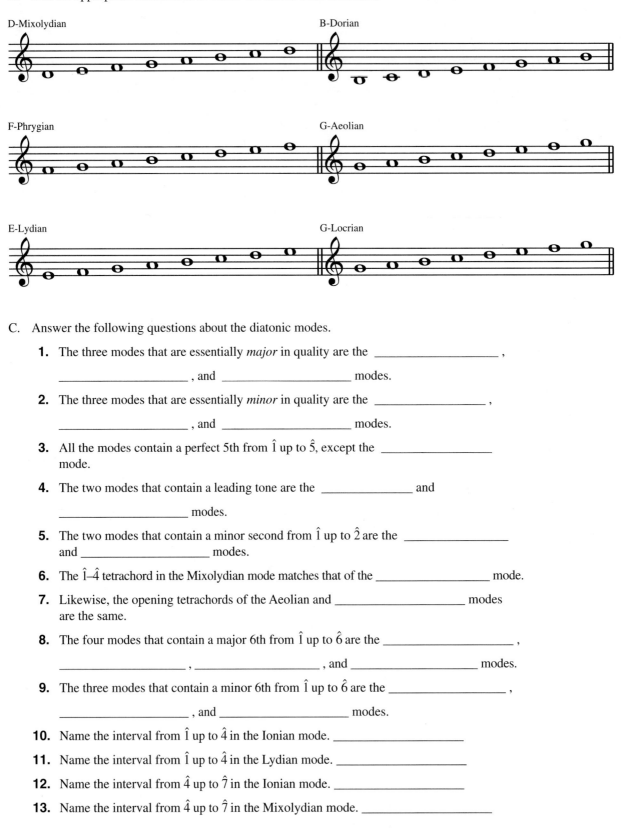

C. Answer the following questions about the diatonic modes.

1. The three modes that are essentially *major* in quality are the _____ , _____ , and _____ modes.

2. The three modes that are essentially *minor* in quality are the _____ , _____ , and _____ modes.

3. All the modes contain a perfect 5th from $\hat{1}$ up to $\hat{5}$, except the _____ mode.

4. The two modes that contain a leading tone are the _____ and _____ modes.

5. The two modes that contain a minor second from $\hat{1}$ up to $\hat{2}$ are the _____ and _____ modes.

6. The $\hat{1}$–$\hat{4}$ tetrachord in the Mixolydian mode matches that of the _____ mode.

7. Likewise, the opening tetrachords of the Aeolian and _____ modes are the same.

8. The four modes that contain a major 6th from $\hat{1}$ up to $\hat{6}$ are the _____ , _____ , _____ , and _____ modes.

9. The three modes that contain a minor 6th from $\hat{1}$ up to $\hat{6}$ are the _____ , _____ , and _____ modes.

10. Name the interval from $\hat{1}$ up to $\hat{4}$ in the Ionian mode. _____

11. Name the interval from $\hat{1}$ up to $\hat{4}$ in the Lydian mode. _____

12. Name the interval from $\hat{4}$ up to $\hat{7}$ in the Ionian mode. _____

13. Name the interval from $\hat{4}$ up to $\hat{7}$ in the Mixolydian mode. _____

D. Using a key signature (rather than appropriate accidentals), notate the following modal scales in the clef indicated.

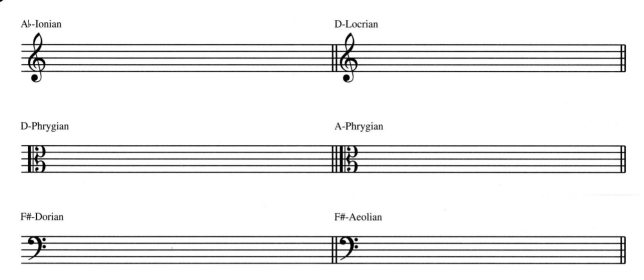

Ab-Ionian   D-Locrian

D-Phrygian   A-Phrygian

F#-Dorian   F#-Aeolian

E. Notate the following pentatonic and synthetic scales starting on the pitch indicated. Be sure to include the octave-related pitch.

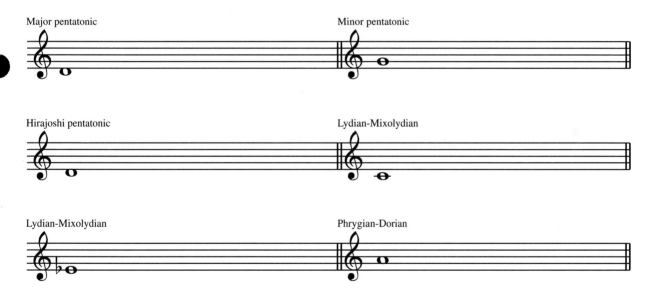

Major pentatonic   Minor pentatonic

Hirajoshi pentatonic   Lydian-Mixolydian

Lydian-Mixolydian   Phrygian-Dorian

F. Notate the following symmetrical scales starting on the pitch indicated. Be sure to
    include the octave-related pitch.

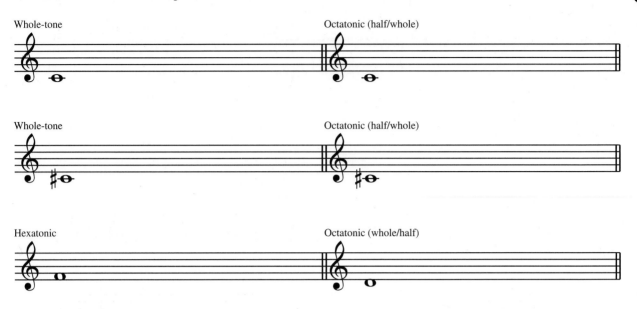

G. Add the appropriate accidentals (or delete the appropriate notes) to create the scale
    indicated. You may choose a starting pitch of B or B♭.

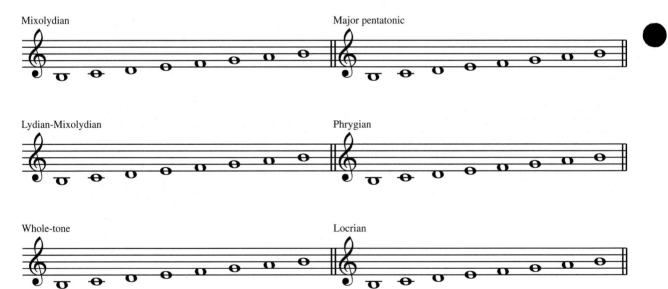

H. Identify the scale used in the following passages.

1   ♩ = ca. 84

_____

DISK: 2 TRACK: 47

2   Allegretto

_____

DISK: 2 TRACK: 48

3   Moderato

_____

4

5

6 Moderately

I.   Analysis. The following examples represent three versions of the principal tune from
     Debussy's "Fêtes." For each, identify the scale being used.

Debussy's "Fêtes," from *Nocturnes* (piano reduction)

scale: _____

scale: _____

Used by permission of Edward B. Marks Music Co.

mm. 29–32

f legato

p il basso staccato

scale: _____

Name ______________________ Class ____________ Date ____________

J. Composition.

Using the major pentatonic scale B♭–C–D–F–G–B♭ as a basis, compose five brief melodies, each of which in turn establishes the indicated tone as a tone center. (Hint: D is tough. Why?)

1

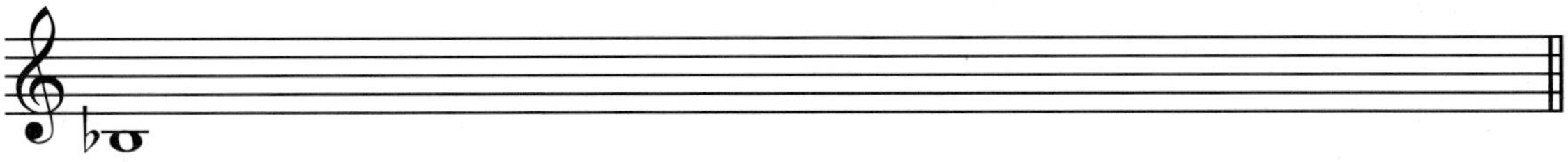

2

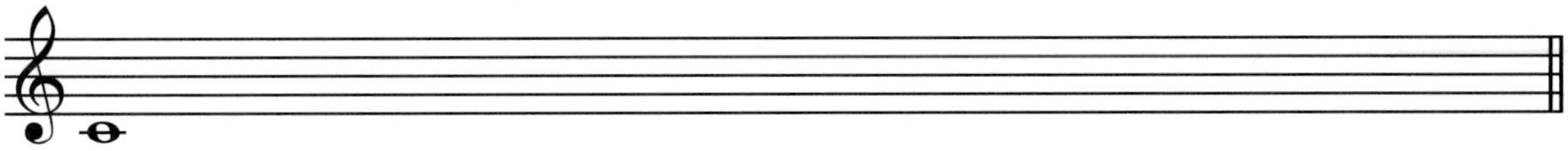

3

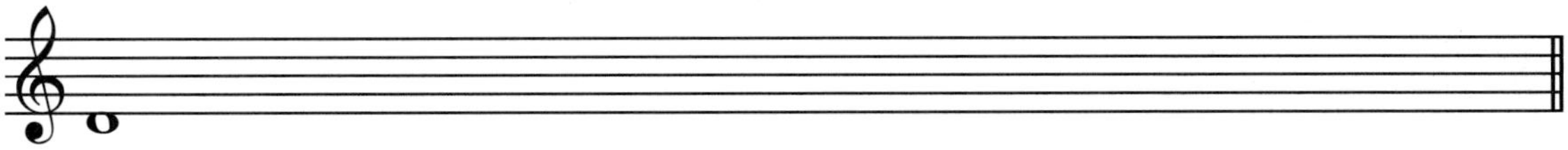

4

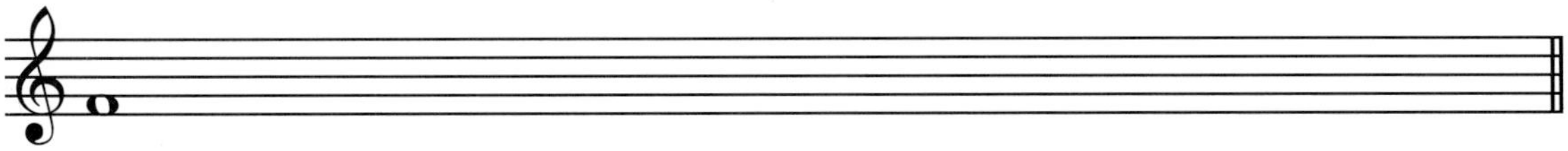

5

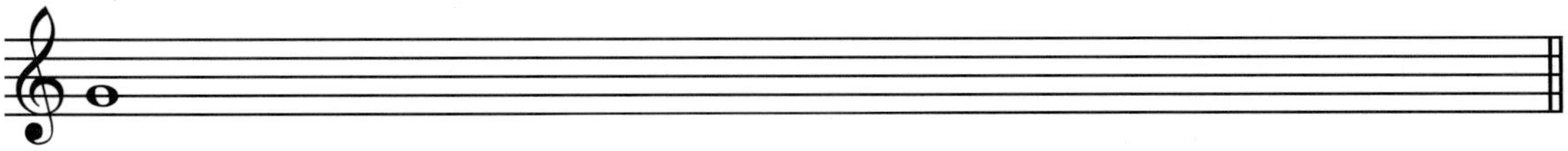

Create a melody based on the octatonic scale that emphasizes major and minor 3rds.
Carefully use rhythmic interest to create an exciting melody.

6

Create a melody based on the hexatonic scale that emphasizes major and minor triads.
Carefully use rhythmic interest to create an exciting melody.

7

Create a two-voice composition based on a whole-tone or octatonic scale. You might want to create a symmetrical relationship between the two voices or perhaps treat them imitatively. If your composition is for piano, experiment with the wide range of the keyboard.

8

EXERCISE 28–2

A. Describe the structure of the following chords by providing the correct symbol: use the symbol "Q" for quartal/quintal chords, "S" for secundal chords, and lead-sheet symbols for tertian sonorities and polychords.

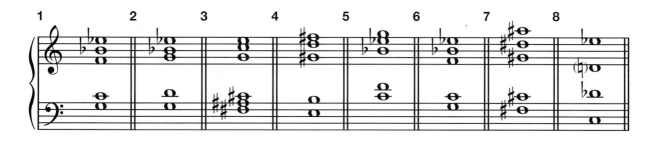

B. Identify the following sonorities as a quartal/quintal chord (Q), split-third chord (ST), whole-tone chord (WT), or tone cluster (TC).

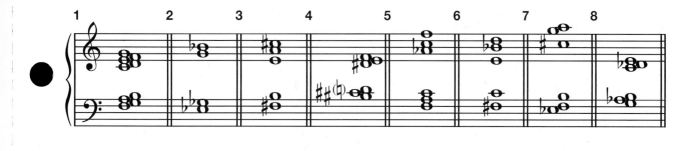

C. Describe the types of vertical sonorities found in the following examples as tertian, polychordal, quartal, quintal, or added-note.

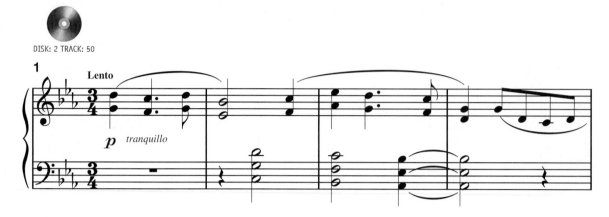

DISK: 2 TRACK: 50

DISK: 2 TRACK: 51

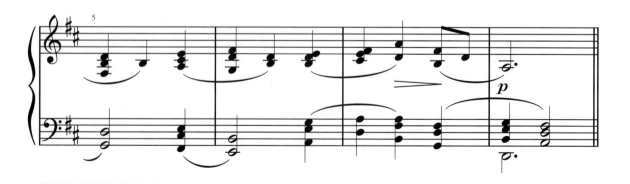

DISK: 2 TRACK: 52

3

DISK: 2 TRACK: 53

4

D. Complete the following passages using chromatic planing. That is, use the given initial sonority to create a passage where all voices move in the same direction by the same interval.

1

2

3

4

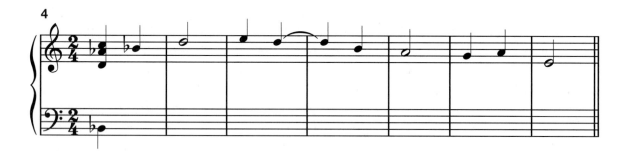

5

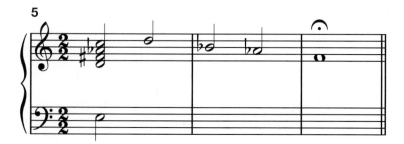

E. Complete the following passages using diatonic planing. That is, use the given initial sonority to create a passage where all voices move in the same direction by the same diatonic interval within the key signature indicated.

1

2

3

4

5

F.   Complete the following passages, using the triad type indicated for each hand. Continue
     the scoring suggested by the first polychord, using the given outer parts consistently as
     either roots, 3rds, or 5ths of the sonority.

1 R.H. major, L.H. major

2 R.H. minor, L.H. minor

3 R.H. major, L.H. minor

4 R.H. major, L.H. minor

G. Analysis. Listen to the following example and answer the following questions.

 1. What technique is used to create form in this piano composition?

    _____

 2. Notate the scale that forms the basis of the opening *four* measures:

    _____

    Does the piece have a tone center? _____ If so, what is it? _____

    If you do not perceive one, why? _____

 3. What are the distinguishing characteristics of the opening two measures? _____

    _____

    _____

 4. In what ways is the character of the opening maintained throughout the piece?

    _____

    _____

 5. What is the derivation of the thematic gesture found in m. 3 of the right-hand part?

    _____ Locate three other instances in which that intervallic pattern
    appears (other than in the bass line).

    a. _____

    b. _____

    c. _____

Payne, *Arch*

H. Composition. With the help of your instructor, execute one or more of the following composition projects. Take great care in the preparation of your score and prepare a performance for class.

    1. Compose a short piece that features extended tertian harmony—for example, ninth, eleventh, and thirteenth chords.

    2. Compose a short piece that features quartal harmony.

    3. Compose a short piece that blends tertian, added-tone, and quartal harmonies.

    4. Compose a short piece that features whole-tone chords.

    5. Compose a short piece that features polychords.

    6. Compose a short piece that features a variety of sonorities derived from a major pentatonic scale.

    7. Compose a short piece that features chromatic-mediant relationships or polychords derived from the octatonic scale.

    8. Compose a short piece that features traditional triads and seventh chords derived from the octatonic scale.

    9. Compose a short piece based on diatonic planing, chromatic planing, or mixed planing.

    10. Compose a short piece that illustrates the principles of pandiatonicism.

EXERCISE 28–3

A. Which of the following rhythmic procedures—added value, asymmetric meter, displaced accent, metric modulation, mixed meter, or nonretrogradable rhythm—are illustrated by the following examples:

1

_____

2

_____

3

_____

4

_____

5

_____

6

_____

B. Messiaen's rhythmic procedures.

    1. Which of the following rhythms are nonretrogradable?

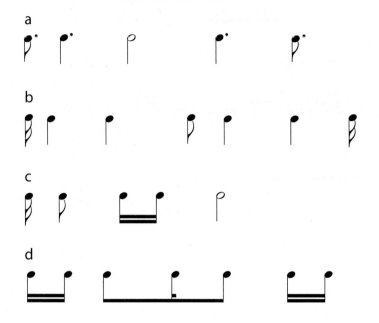

    2. Consider the rhythmic figure:

Identify the added value in the following rhythms by marking it with a "+" symbol.

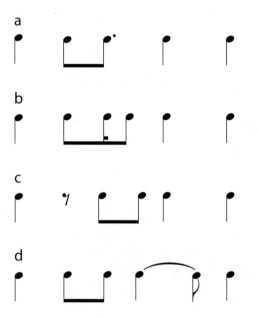

Name _____ Class _____ Date _____

C. Answer the following questions about the terms and concepts mentioned in the Rhythm and Meter section of Chapter 28.

1. _____ is an interaction between rhythm and meter that implies a 3:2 ratio.

2. Music that lacks an aurally perceivable meter is called _____ music.

3. The simultaneous presentation of two or more strikingly contrasted rhythmic streams is called _____.

4. _____ rhythm refers to the listener's perception that unequal groupings of subdivisions are being added together.

5. A _____ bar line can be used to indicate irregular subdivisions of the bar.

6. Traditional meters, such as $\frac{4}{4}, \frac{2}{4}, \frac{3}{4}, \frac{6}{8}$, etc., are often referred to as _____ meters because they are based on regular recurring pulses that are subdivided into groups of two or three.

7. A musical pattern that is repeated many times in succession is called an

    _____.

8. A modern term for a rhythmic technique associated with Medieval motets and masses, an _____ typically consists of a repeated rhythmic figure called the _____ in combination with a repeated pitch sequence of a different length called the

    _____.

9. An immediate change in tempo created by equating a particular note value to another note value, a proportional note value, usually located in the next bar is called a _____

    _____.

10. The Fibonacci sequence is an infinite sequence of numbers that can be written, for example,

    1, 1, 2, 3, _____,_____,_____,_____,_____,_____, 89, etc.

11. Each member of the Fibonacci sequence is the sum of the previous _____ numbers.

12. The consecutive ratios implied by the Fibonacci sequence—for example, 3:2, 5:3, 8:5, 13:8, etc.—approach the _____ _____ (ca. 1.618:1), a proportion found throughout nature that has also been associated with proportional balance in art and architecture.

13. The point approximately .618 of the way through a piece where the climax of the work or other important musical event occurs is called the _____

    _____.

14. The simultaneous use of two or more strikingly contrasted tempos is called

    _____.

15. A canon in which the individual voices are presented at different tempos is called a

    _____ _____.

D. Analysis. Comment on the rhythmic and metric devices employed in the following
   excerpts.

1   **Maestoso**

Stravinsky, "Danse de la foire," from *Petrouchka* (piano reduction)

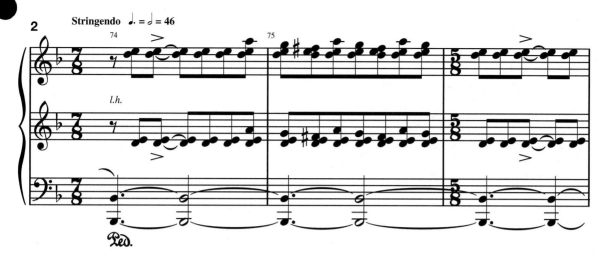

Used by permission of Edward B. Marks Music Co.

E. Composition. With the help of your instructor, execute one or more of the following composition projects. Take great care in the preparation of your score and prepare a performance for class.

1. Create a polyrhythmic composition for two percussionists. Use any two like nonpitched percussion instruments (claves, cowbells, hand-claps, etc.).

2. Create a composition for any two instruments that features a passage based on polymeter.

3. Create a composition that utilizes two or more of the following rhythmic devices: added value, asymmetric meter, displaced accent, metric modulation, or mixed meter.

Chapter 29

POST-TONAL THEORY

EXERCISE 29–1

A. Mod 12 and Pitch Class. Reduce the following integers to an integer mod 12 (0 to 11 inclusive). Use the pc clockface diagram to aid in your calculations.

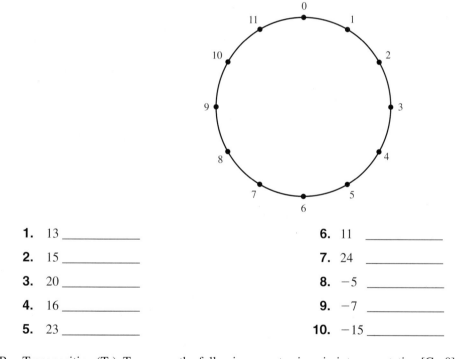

1. 13 _____

2. 15 _____

3. 20 _____

4. 16 _____

5. 23 _____

6. 11 _____

7. 24 _____

8. −5 _____

9. −7 _____

10. −15 _____

B. Transposition (T_n). Transpose the following pc sets given in integer notation [C=0].

1. T_1 (1,2,3) = _____

2. T_3 (3,6,9) = _____

3. T_6 (7,5,3) = _____

4. T_5 (11,6,1) = _____

5. T_0 (2,9,7) = _____

6. T_8 (2,6,10) = _____

7. T_2 (7,5,3,1) = _____

8. T_9 (3,6,9,0) = _____

9. T_4 (8,0,1,3) = _____

10. T_7 (7,1,6,0) = _____

C. Inversion (T_nI). Invert the following pc sets given in integer notation [C=0]. Use the two-step procedure shown in the following example.*

	Operation	Set After PC Inversion	Answer
Example	$T_{10}I$ (8,6,5) =	T_{10} (4,6,7) =	(2,4,5)
1.	T_6I (1,2,4) =	T_6(____,____,____) =	(____,____,____)
2.	T_9I (7,8,9) =	T_9(____,____,____) =	(____,____,____)
3.	$T_{11}I$ (11,8,7) =	T_{11}(____,____,____) =	(____,____,____)
4.	T_1I (11,8,7) =	T_1(____,____,____) =	(____,____,____)
5.	T_5I (10,9,0,11) =	T_5(____,____,____,____) =	(____,____,____,____)
6.	T_0I (4,6,5,9) =	T_0(____,____,____,____) =	(____,____,____,____)
7.	T_7I (1,0,7,6) =	T_7(____,____,____,____) =	(____,____,____,____)
8.	T_4I (2,6,8,4) =	T_4(____,____,____,____) =	(____,____,____,____)

*Note that the T_nI operation may also be performed using a one-step procedure. The procedure involves subtracting each member of the set in turn from the index n of T_nI, for instance, in the preceding example:

Operation	One-Step Procedure	Answer
$T_{10}I$ (8,6,5) =	(10-8,10-6,10-5) =	(2,4,5)

D. Interval Class. Provide the interval class names of the following intervals by using the numbers 0 through 6.

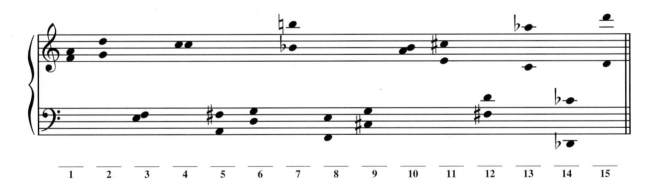

E. Interval Vector. Label each interval in the given pc set using interval classes. Use this information to identify the set's interval vector.

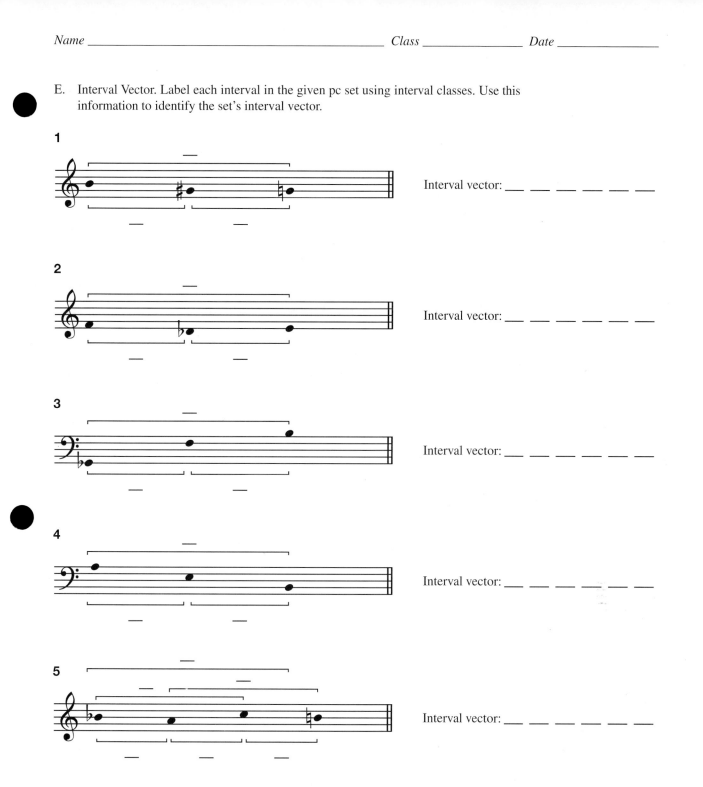

1

Interval vector: __ __ __ __ __ __

2

Interval vector: __ __ __ __ __ __

3

Interval vector: __ __ __ __ __ __

4

Interval vector: __ __ __ __ __ __

5

Interval vector: __ __ __ __ __ __

F. Notate the given pc set using staff notation in the space provided. Then determine the
    set's normal form and prime form.

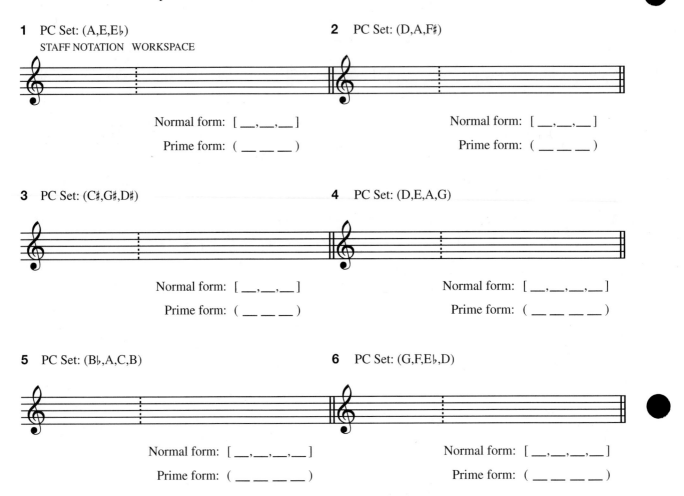

1 PC Set: (A,E,E♭)

STAFF NOTATION WORKSPACE

Normal form: [__,__,__]

Prime form: (__ __ __)

2 PC Set: (D,A,F♯)

Normal form: [__,__,__]

Prime form: (__ __ __)

3 PC Set: (C♯,G♯,D♯)

Normal form: [__,__,__]

Prime form: (__ __ __)

4 PC Set: (D,E,A,G)

Normal form: [__,__,__,__]

Prime form: (__ __ __ __)

5 PC Set: (B♭,A,C,B)

Normal form: [__,__,__,__]

Prime form: (__ __ __ __)

6 PC Set: (G,F,E♭,D)

Normal form: [__,__,__,__]

Prime form: (__ __ __ __)

G. For each of the following sonorities (trichords and tetrachords), determine the normal form, prime form, Forte name, and interval vector.

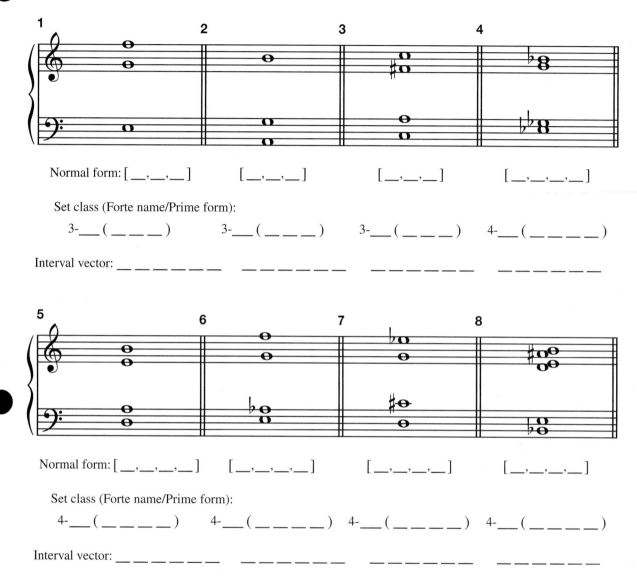

Normal form: [__,__,__]   [__,__,__]   [__,__,__]   [__,__,__,__]

Set class (Forte name/Prime form):

3-___ (__ __ __)   3-___ (__ __ __)   3-___ (__ __ __)   4-___ (__ __ __ __)

Interval vector: __ __ __ __ __ __   __ __ __ __ __ __   __ __ __ __ __ __   __ __ __ __ __ __

Normal form: [__,__,__,__]   [__,__,__,__]   [__,__,__,__]   [__,__,__,__]

Set class (Forte name/Prime form):

4-___ (__ __ __ __)   4-___ (__ __ __ __)   4-___ (__ __ __ __)   4-___ (__ __ __ __)

Interval vector: __ __ __ __ __ __   __ __ __ __ __ __   __ __ __ __ __ __   __ __ __ __ __ __

H. Analysis. *From Ritual to Romance* for solo piano by Reginald Bain, which follows, opens with an atonal passage. Try to play the example and then answer the following questions:

1. Determine the normal form of the initial four-note melodic gesture (C,C♯,G,F♯). To what set class does this pc set belong?

    Normal form: [__, __, __, __] Belongs to set class: 4-__ (__ __ __ __)

2. Find two other melodic instances of this set class in the passage. Circle these occurrences on the score and mark them with the appropriate Forte name.

3. The three-note melodic cell (G,F♯,B♭) plays an important role in the passage. Determine this set's normal form. To what set class does it belong?

    Normal form: [__, __, __] Belongs to set class: 3-__ (__ __ __)

4. Find four instances of this set class in m. 6. Circle them on the score and mark them with the appropriate Forte name.

5. Determine the normal form of the chord (B,E,B♭), which occurs in the right hand, m. 2. To what set class does it belong?

    Normal form: [__, __, __] Belongs to set class: 3-__ (__ __ __)

6. Find another instance of this set class in the right hand. Circle it on the score and mark it with the appropriate Forte name.

7. To what interval class does the left hand gesture in m. 2 belong?

    ic___

    Is this interval class prominently featured in the set classes you identified above?

    Yes/No (circle one)

8. A new set class begins to play an important role in m. 5. Two occurrences may be found in the right-hand melody, mm. 5–6. What set class is it?

    Set class: 3-__ (__ __ __)

    Circle both occurrences on the score and mark them with the appropriate Forte name.

Bain, *From Ritual to Romance*

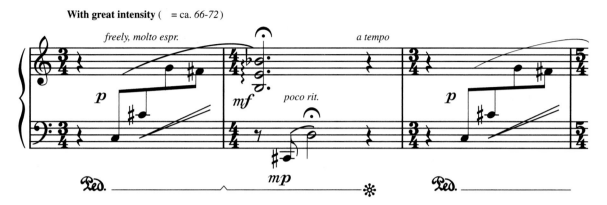

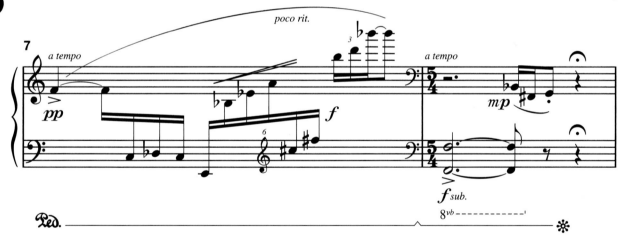

From Ritual to Romance for solo piano by Reginald Bain. © 1985 Reginald Bain. Used by permission of Tractatus Edition.

I.   Composition. Compose a piece according to one of the following specifications and prepare a performance for class.

1.   Create a melody that begins with a statement of set class 3-1 (012) and goes on to emphasize the following interval classes: ic2 (e.g., M2 or m7), ic1 (e.g., m2 or M7) and ic5 (e.g., P4 or P5).

2.   Create a composition for piano that is based on two harmonic cells and two melodic cells. For example, you might choose set classes 3-9 (027) and 3-7 (025) for your harmonic cells and ic1 and ic2 for your melodic cells.

EXERCISE 29-2

A. The series given below is from Berg's *Lyric Suite*. Given the P_0 form of the series, notate the I_0 form on the staff provided, then complete the 12×12 matrix. Label the series forms using the blanks provided.

B. Answer the following questions about the structure of the series from Berg's *Lyric Suite*.

1. In the following trichordal segmentation of the series, identify the set class to which each discrete trichord belongs by providing its Forte name and prime form.

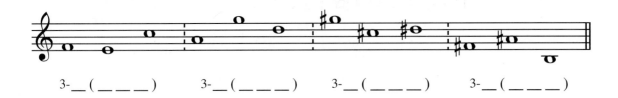

3-__ (__ __ __)   3-__ (__ __ __)   3-__ (__ __ __)   3-__ (__ __ __)

2. In the following tetrachordal segmentation of the series, identify the set class to which each discrete tetrachord belongs by providing its Forte name and prime form.

4-__ (__ __ __ __)   4-__ (__ __ __ __)   4-__ (__ __ __ __)

3. Determine the normal order of the two discrete hexachords.

                1st Hexachord   2nd Hexachord
Normal order: [__, __, __, __, __, __]   [__, __, __, __, __, __]

From what scale do the two hexachords appear to be derived? The _____ scale.

4. Examine the intervallic structure of the series by filling in the blanks to indicate the number of semitones up to the next pitch class. For example, F–E is up 11 semitones.

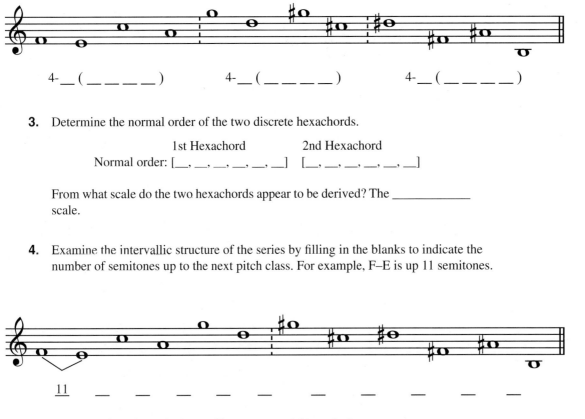

<u>11</u>   __   __   __   __   __   __   __   __   __   __

What is interesting about the intervallic structure of this series? _____

_____

C. Series Forms. Given the P$_0$ form of the series from Schoenberg's *Fourth String Quartet,* op. 37:

notate the following series forms. The first note has been done for you.

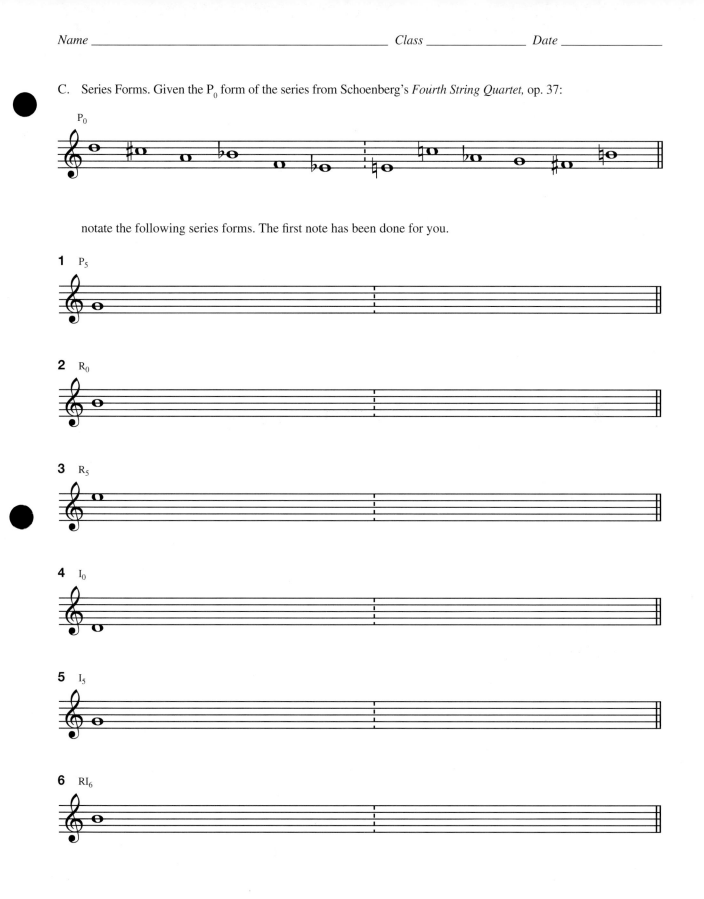

D. Analysis

1. "Full Moon" by Otto Joachim is based on a 12-tone series. It employs a single series form that we will call P_0. First, identify the series and notate it (using the treble clef) on the staff provided. (Hint: The series is presented for the first time in mm. 1–3. The order of the pitch classes in m. 3 is E♭–B♭–G♭–D♭.)

P_0

Order
numbers: 1   2   3   4   5   6   7   8   9   10   11   12

Now trace the presentation of the series in mm. 1–24 by marking series form symbols (remember, the piece employs only P_0) and order numbers (1–12) on the score.

Full Moon

Otto Joachim

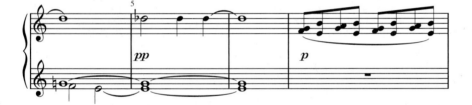

from *Twelve 12-Tone Pieces for Children*
© Copyright 1961 by BMI Canada Ltd. Copyright assigned 1969 to Berandol Music Ltd. Scarborough.

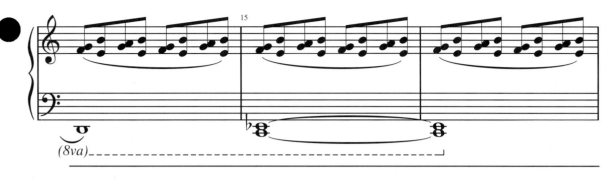

In some ways, "Full Moon" sounds almost impressionistic. What compositional devices has the composer employed to create this effect?

_____

_____

_____

2. "The Moon Rises" by Ernst Krenek is based on the following 12-tone series:

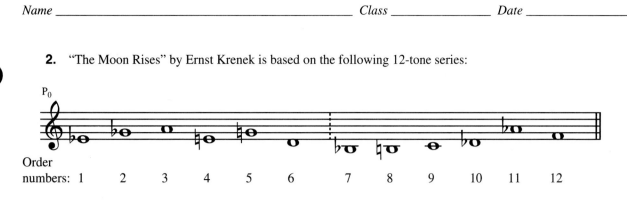

Order
numbers: 1   2   3   4   5   6   7   8   9   10   11   12

Like Joachim's "Full Moon," it employs a single series form (P_0). Trace the presentation of the series throughout the course of the piece by marking series form symbols and order numbers (1–12) on the score.

Krenek, "The Moon Rises," from *Twelve Short Piano Pieces*, op. 83

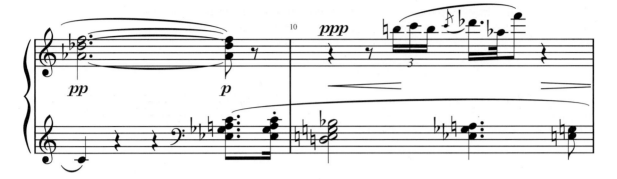

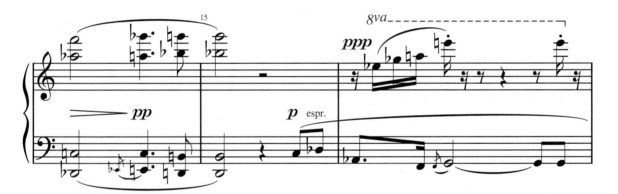

3. "Glass Figures" by Ernst Krenek, is based on the following 12-tones series. In preparation for the work that follows, notate the I_0 and R_0 forms of the series on the staves
provided:

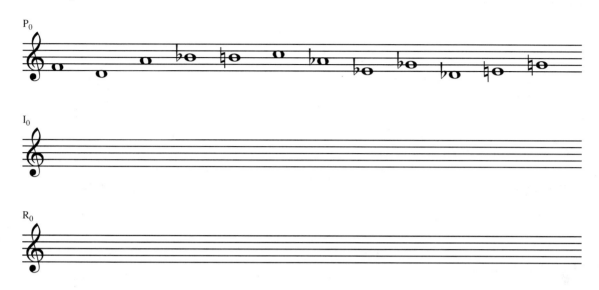

In examining the music, you will note that the first measure of the right hand opens
with the first three notes of I_0, whereas the left hand features the first two notes of R_0.
The third note of this latter series form is $D^\flat$. It is accommodated by the right hand because the third note of I_0 is also a $D\flat$. Following this, the roles of the series forms are
reversed, with the left hand picking up I_0 while the right hand continues with R_0. Because of the frequency of this type of exchange where two or more series forms are involved, it is advisable to use different-colored pencils to indicate different series forms
in operation.

Krenek, "Glass Figures," from *Twelve Short Piano Pieces*. op. 83

"Glass Figures" from *Twelve Short Piano Pieces* by Ernst Krenek. Copyright © 1939 (renewed) by Associated Music Publishers, Inc. (BMI). International copyright secured. All rights reserved. Reprinted
by permission.

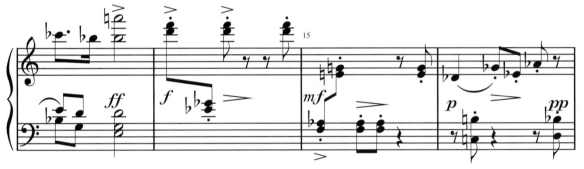

Name ______________________ *Class* __________ *Date* __________

E. Composition. Using the series for "The Moon Rises" shown next, compose a two-voice composition, the upper voice of which is based on a transposed series form while the lower voice makes use of a retrograde series form. You might want to try using instruments other than piano, such as violin and cello or two flutes.

P_0

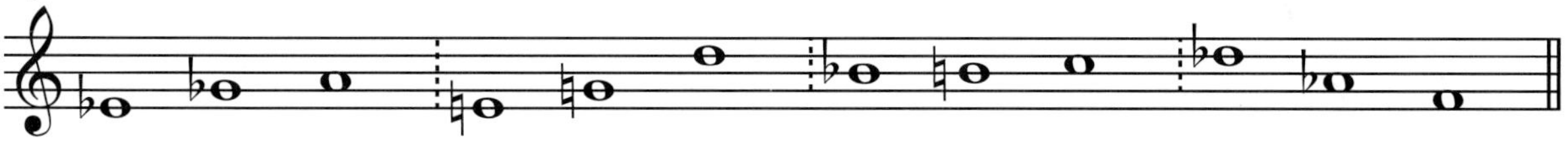

EXERCISE 29–3

A. Answer the following questions about integral serialism.

   1. The term *total serialization* refers to the process whereby parameters other than pitch, such as _____ , _____, and _____, are decided on by means of a predetermined series.

   2. Two composers associated with the origins of total serialization are _____ and _____.

   3. The French composer _____ composed *Structures Ia* (1952), a work whose pitch series was adapted from Messiaen's *Mode de valeurs et d'intensités* (1949).

   4. The American composer _____ was evidently the first to explore the serialization of elements other than pitch in *Three Compositions for Piano* (1947).

B. Analysis.

   1. With the help of your instructor, find a work that illustrates the principles of integral serialism. Analyze and write a summary of the work.

C. Composition.

   1. Compose a short piece featuring elements of total serialization. Prepare a performance for class.

Chapter 30

NEW DIRECTIONS

EXERCISE 30–1

A. Answer the following questions about the terms and concepts mentioned in Chapter 30.

1. John Cage composed works for _____ _____ that involved the placement of various objects and/or materials on the strings of the piano at precisely specified locations.

2. The system of tuning in which the intervals are represented using whole-number ratios is called _____ _____.

3. The interval that divides the octave into 24 equal parts is called the _____ _____.

4. The scores for George Crumb's *Makrokosmos* and Krzysztof Penderecki's *Threnody to the Victims of Hiroshima* are examples of _____ _____, a notational style that uses nontraditional symbols to represent musical information.

5. _____ _____ is a notational style that indicates approximate durations through the spacing of events and timings.

6. Compositions created out of sound masses distinguished not by pitch but by timbre, rhythm, density, register, and so forth are called _____-_____ _____.

7. György Ligeti used the term _____ to describe the canonic relationships between the voices in the complex, clusterlike surfaces of his early orchestral works.

8. The extended vocal technique associated with Arnold Schoenberg's *Pierrot lunaire* is called _____, a cross between singing and dramatic declamation.

9. Gunther Schuller led a movement called _____-_____ which blended elements of jazz and serious contemporary music.

10. _____ or _____ refers to music in which elements of a composition have intentionally been left undetermined by the composer.

11. In *Music of Changes* (1951) for solo piano, John Cage used _____ _____ derived from the *I Ching,* the ancient Chinese *Book of Changes,* to determine the work's pitches, durations, dynamics, and so forth.

12. John Cage helped to initiate the _____ _____ tradition with works such as *Imaginary Landscape No. 4* (1951) for 12 radios and *4′ 33″* (1952).

13. The term _____ refers to a style that seems to have evolved out of the music of John Cage and Morton Feldman and is characterized by a return to tonal elements and diatonicism, as well as the use of restricted pitch materials, static harmony, and rhythmic elements inspired by Eastern music.

14. The concept of _____ is a compositional process associated with the music of Steve Reich in which two identical copies of a musical pattern are allowed to drift out of phase with one another. The rich surface texture that results is essentially the product of unforeseen _____ _____ that are created by the constantly shifting relationship between the parts.

15. Examples of early electronic instruments include the _____, _____ _____, and _____.

16. Music that exists primarily in the medium of magnetic tape is called _____ _____.

17. Pierre Schaeffer's approach to electronic music in which he worked directly with recorded sounds, organizing them into musical structures without the use of traditional notation, is called _____ _____.

18. The _____ _____ _____ spans ca. 20 Hz. to 20,000 Hz.

19. An _____ _____ gives musical shape to an oscillator's static tone by imparting an attack, decay, sustain, and release phase to the tone's overall loudness profile.

20. The introduction of _____ _____ _____ in the 1960s marketed under trade names of Moog, Buchla, and ARP, offered a wide palette of new electronic sounds.

21. Released in 1983, the Yamaha DX-7 was one of the first commercially successful _____. It was based on an _____ _____ technique discovered by John Chowning at Stanford in the late 1960s.

22. A software application that stores sequences of MIDI data is called a _____.

23. Iannis Xenakis is perhaps best known for his _____ _____, in which the musical parameters such as pitch, intensity, and duration are determined by the laws of probability theory.

24. Tod Machover coined the term _____ to refer to his use of computers to augment musical expression and creativity.

25. The underlying tonal basis of many of Paul Lansky's computer-generated compositions has caused some to describe these complex works as a form of _____, a term used to refer to music that seems to have its roots in the minimalist traditions of the 1960s and 1970s.

B. Analysis. With the help of your instructor and appropriate secondary sources:

  1. Find a work that illustrates the use of expanded textural, timbral, or tuning resources. Analyze and write a summary of the piece.

  2. Find a work that illustrates the principles of indeterminacy. Analyze and write a summary of the piece.

  3. Find a work that illustrates the principles of minimalism. Analyze and write a summary of the piece.

  4. Find a work that illustrates the principles of the new vocalism. Analyze and write a summary of the piece.

  5. Find a work that is an example of *musique concrète*. Analyze and write a summary of the piece.

  6. Find a work that is, strictly speaking, an example of electronic music. Analyze and write a summary of the piece.

  7. Find a work that uses electronic means of any sort to reinterpret a work by a well-known Baroque, Classical, or Romantic composer. Analyze and write a summary of the piece.

  8. Find a work that combines live performer and recorded music (tape, cd, etc.) or real-time interaction with a computer. Analyze and write a summary of the piece.

C. Composition. With the help of your instructor, execute one or more of the following composition projects. Take great care in the preparation of your score and performance directions. Prepare a performance for class.

  1. Compose a short piece featuring aleatoric or indeterminate elements.

  2. Compose a short piece featuring special effects for your instrument or voice.

  3. Compose a short piece with a nontraditional score that features both graphic and proportional notation.

  4. Compose a short piece that is based on an alternative tuning system (quarter tones, just intonation, etc.).

  5. Compose a short piece that features tone clusters and that is based on the principles of sound-mass composition.

  6. Compose a short piece that blends elements of jazz and serious contemporary music.

  7. Compose a short minimalist piece based on the concept of phasing. Use a one-measure melodic gesture as the basis for the work.

  8. Compose a short electronic composition using music software that is freely available over the Internet.

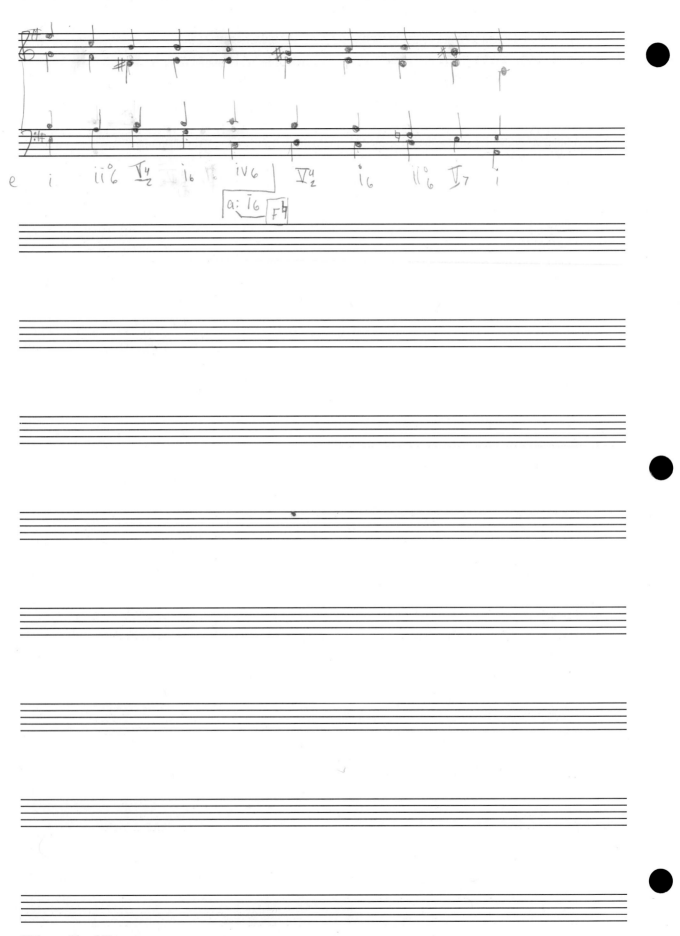

e   i   ii°6 V^4_2 i6 i6 iV6 V^4_2 i6   ii°6 V_7 i

a: $\overline{\text{i}}$6 F♮

Name _____ Class _____ Date _____

Compact Discs to Accompany Workbook

THE PERFORMERS

Jana Holzmeier, Jennifer Murray, *soprano*
Julia Armstrong, *mezzo-soprano*
Tim Campbell, David L. Jones, David Stevens, *tenor*
Joel Quade, David Small, Richard Womack, *baritone*
Elizabeth Whitten, *flute*
David Pinkard, *bassoon*
Michael Misner, James Wester, *horn*
Jennifer Bourianoff, Marian Mentel, Colleen
    McCullough, *violin*
Kyle Sigrest, Reuben Allred, *piano*
David Mead, Alejandro Hernandez-Valdez, *piano and
    harpsichord*
Roger Graybill, Lenore Alford, *organ*
Myra Spector, Tina Marsh, *jazz vocals*
David Renter, *jazz saxophone*
Jeff Hellmer, Anthony Belfiglio, *jazz piano*
Kris Afflerbaugh, *jazz bass*

The Barton Strings
Beth Blackerby, *violin*
Jennifer Bourianoff, *violin and viola*
Martha Carapetyan, Bruce Williams, *viola*
Carolyn Blubaugh-Hagler, *violoncello*

Tosca String Quartet
Leigh Mahoney, *1st violin*
Tracy Seeger Beth Blackerby, *2nd violin*
Ames Asbell, *viola*
Sara Nelson, *cello*

Chamber Choir—David Mead, *conductor*
Judith Kanana, Carol Hopkins, *soprano*
Brooke Lehr, Kellie McCurdy, *contralto*
Oliver Worthington, *tenor*

Te Oti Rakena, Steven Olivares, *bass*
Orchestra—David Mead, Alejandro Hernandez
    Valdez, *conductors*
Elizabeth Whitten, Michelle Clover Neal, *flute*
Pamela Whitcomb, Lana Neal, *oboe*
Marisa Bannworth Wester, Shannon Thompson,
    clarinet
David Pinkard, Rhonda Collison, *bassoon*
James Wester, Michael Misner, Richard
    Wheatley, Kellie Babcock, *horn*
Thomas Caswell, Stephen Miles, *trumpet*
Sean Scot Reed, David Garcia, David
    Hendricksen, *trombone*
Richard Short, *timpani*
Marian Mentel, *concertmaster*; Tera Shimizu,
    principal violin II
Jennifer Fedie, Wei He, Daniel McAtee, Sean
    Milligan, Hye-Sung Oh, Sue-Jean Park,
    Linda Piatt, Thomas Sender, Marvin
    Suson, Alicija Usarek, *violin*
Joseph Tan, Mark Sattler, Jason Elinoff, *viola*
Paul Rhodes, Kirsten Eggen, Sara Nelson,
    Victorial Wolff, *violoncello*
John Rosenkrans, Robert Jenkins, *contrabass*

Mark Ellis, *announcer*
David Mead, Alejandro Hernandez–Valdez, Anthony
    Suter, Andrew Murphy, *producers*
Andrew Murphy, Frank Simon, *engineers*
J. Burke Hunn, Michael Czysz, *assistant
    engineers*

Recorded at the School of Music, University of
    Texas at Austin